A Prayer for
Burma

Written and Illustrated by
Kenneth Wong

SANTA
MONICA
PRESS

S A N T A
M O N I C A
P R E S S

Published by:
Santa Monica Press LLC
P.O. Box 1076
Santa Monica, CA 90406-1076
1-800-784-9553
www.santamonicapress.com
books@santamonicapress.com

Printed in the United States

Santa Monica Press books are available at special quantity discounts when purchased in bulk by corporations, organizations, or groups. Please call our Special Sales department at 1-800-784-9553.

ISBN 1-891661-28-0

Library of Congress Cataloging-in-Publication Data

Wong, Kenneth, 1968-
    A prayer for Burma / by Kenneth Wong.
      p. cm.
    ISBN 1-891661-28-0
    1. Burma—Description and travel. 2. Burma—Social life and customs.
    3. Wong, Kenneth, 1968—Journeys—Burma. I. Title.

DS527.7.W66 2003
959.105—dc21

                                  2003000336

Book and cover design by Lynda "Cool Dog" Jakovich

Contents

For my childhood friends and the people of Burma

Acknowledgments

A piece of writing is generally the outcome of an author's solitary struggle to overcome his own inner demons. Since he has chosen to participate in this metaphysical wrestling match at nobody's urging, he and he alone must endure the consequences of it. A book, on the other hand, is the product of the labor of numerous individuals who see something worthwhile in a writer's work and choose to encourage him. Hence, the success of a book must be attributed to, and shared by, everyone who has participated, knowingly or unknowingly, in its creation.

First and foremost, I must thank Jeffrey Goldman, the publisher at Santa Monica Press; without his spirit of adventure, this book would have probably remained a crumpled manuscript hidden in the back of my draw. I am grateful to my parents and my beloved sister; they make enormous personal sacrifices to accommodate my obstinate insistence on independence and isolation—two luxuries rarely permissible in an Asian family.

I am indebted to my dear friends Heidi and Vicky: they prevented many misplaced commas and misappropriated words from ever appearing in print; they both helped me make critical editorial decisions; and they did all these for no more than the promise of a free meal. I must also acknowledge my literary comrades, Jonathan, Laura, and Shanna, for their unwavering support in all my literary endeavors small and great; at times, they have more faith in me than I have in myself.

I will be remiss if I do not credit my colleagues at CADENCE magazine; they are the craziest, nuttiest, silliest bunch of editors ever assembled and they inspire me more than they'll ever know. There are also the editors, copyeditors, proofreaders, designers, and other professional men and women involved in the physical production of the book; to each of them, I send my warmest wishes and thanks.

Finally, I'd like to pay homage to Aung San Suu Kyi, the leader of the Burmese democratic movement, who is the answer to Burma's prayer for liberty and justice. In time she shall prevail, and so shall the people of Burma.

Kenneth Wong

The Foreigner and the Native

I used to attend lectures in the intolerable June heat with a hand-woven ceremonial sarong wrapped around my waist and a long-sleeved collar-less shirt buttoned to my neck. All the lecture halls in Rangoon University were nostalgically named after the legendary kingdoms of medieval Burma. I recall two in particular: *Sagaing* and *Taungu*. All of them, as if to evoke the memory of the fallen dynasties they were named after, emitted a stale smell similar to that of ancient dungeons, where condemned nobles and dethroned monarchs waiting to be hung or decapitated spent their final days. Lighting was minimal; the small windows did little to welcome the occasional breezes that fondled the tamarind trees outside.

Trapped in those grim chambers, the students combated the stifling heat using various ingenious methods: some unbuttoned their shirts as far down as it was permissible; others fanned themselves with their textbooks; and the girls, for whom unbuttoning was not an option because they were held to a higher standard of modesty, strategically positioned themselves near doorways, which not only admitted a vast amount of air but also permitted a quick retreat when threatened by suffocation or dehydration. It was not required, nor was it advisable, to dress as I did. But I was fastidiously concerned with the preservation of dignity so I willingly sacrificed comfort for the sake of decorum and stoically endured more than my fair share of this tropical torture.

Returning to Rangoon after living ten years in San Francisco, I confronted once again this familiar but forgotten Burmese heat—something I could no longer endure with the indifference of a native. The fog and the sea breezes of San Francisco had seeped into my limbs. The thermal resistance of my childhood had all but dissolved. Now, anything above room temperature made me uneasy. I had carefully planned to arrive during December, the coldest month of the year, for the expressed purpose of avoiding this heat.

But Burma was unwilling to abide by the seasonal laws; it operated, as it had always done, under a different and peculiar set of rules that were entirely its own. It greeted me with the malicious heat of a witch's boiling cauldron when I stepped out of my room. But I remained as unyielding as I had always been in my obsession with dignity; and, having studied a number of Victorian novels, I was determined not just to cling to dignity but to wear it on my lapel like a conspicuous rose. So I put on a crisp linen shirt and an ostentatious silk tie, and went out to face the venomous heat of my motherland.

Burma, being my birthplace, is definitively and figuratively my motherland—not exactly a lullaby-humming, muffin-baking mother full of reassurances, but an unpredictable and eccentric mother, whose cradle ricocheted like a defective roller coaster more often than it swung like a steady pendulum. America, who embraced me with open arms when I left Burma at the age of twenty-one, may well be my foster father. But there is also old China, whose sepia-toned photo haunts me with his distant eyes whenever I open the family album, for I am ethnically Chinese although I was born in Burma. China is, in a way, the grandfather I can barely remember. My own biological parents are an odd pair of Asian archetypes—my father an armchair-bound Buddhist who accepts everyone, and my mother a headstrong pragmatist who challenges everything. It is not easy to grow up between a serene hermit and a hotheaded materialist. And it is even harder to be the product of a tri-cultural upbringing— with quirky Burma for a mother, liberal America for a foster father, and autocratic China for a grandfather.

My own identity, which is made up of tiny fragments of my national and cultural identities, resembles the vision inside a kaleidoscope—I see a different picture every time I look. I learned early on that a complete understanding of any kind was simply impossible with Burma. But, returning to my motherland, just as an estranged son would to the mother he had left behind, I had hoped to get at least a *better* understanding of this colorful cultural mandala that was my identity.

Kandawgyi, the great lake at the center of Rangoon, was within walking distance from Bagan Inn, my temporary residence. In fact, the lake was the primary reason I had selected this particular establishment. I knew Kandawgyi was one of the few places in the city where fresh air was still available; the air was filled with fumes everywhere else, coughed up by dilapidated trucks and buses (some of which traveled so sluggishly that they were frequently outrun by the pedestrians chasing after them). The sky above Rangoon had turned ashen gray with a thick veil of smog. Pollution seemed to have worsened ten fold within the last ten years. I knew many young Burmese who routinely visited one tea shop after another, smoking cheroots— homemade Burmese cigars—at each because they had little else to do. I thought of urging them to quit, but it seemed silly since the air they were breathing could cause just as much damage to their lungs.

The sun had not yet risen when I came out of the inn. I found the receptionist—a thin man with a melancholy grin—sound asleep in the tiny closet-like room behind the polished teak counter. I woke him up and asked him for directions to Kandawgyi. His speech was incoherent. When I looked confused, he communicated with me in a body language that was entirely of his own—gesturing with his arms and elbows, and pointing with his chin, he showed me how to get there from the inn. I made a mental note of his anatomical directions. I asked him if it was safe to take a walk in the neighborhood at such an early hour. Eyeballing the wallet spilling out of my khaki pants, he reluctantly said, "Yes."

I paused at the intersection, trying to remember the exact angle of the receptionist's elbow. But I was now at different coordinates, facing a different direction. If I were to continue according his anatomical directions (which had begun to fade from my memory), I would need to reconstruct all his bodily gestures from a different perspective. This was too much mental effort for my first morning back. I was on vacation and so was my brain; I wasn't in the mood to solve a complex geometric puzzle. The way I saw it, I could treat the puzzle as a multiple-choice question: (A) Turn left (B) Turn right. So I did what I used to do in high school when I found myself in a similar predicament—I took a guess.

I turned right, which was *not* the way to Kandawgyi. Actually, it *was* the way to Kandawgyi; it just wasn't the best way. There are many mysterious townships in Rangoon where no matter which way one turns, one eventually ends up at one's destination—the only difference is the time it takes. And, for many Burmese, time is something they have in abundance. For some, it is the *only* thing they have in abundance.

I sauntered through the quiet township of Tamwe, which was for the most part still asleep. There were a few exceptions to the sprawling landscape of stillness—a produce merchant setting up shop, a cab driver washing his car, and a team of Buddhist monks collecting alms. The monks walked in single file, led by two stout men shouldering a heavy pole from which hung a regal gong. The novices trotted along at the end of the line, shuffling their saffron robes and bouncing their lacquer bowls. Every once in a while, the two forerunners struck the gong with a short stick, producing a brassy G flat that drove potential benefactors out of their comfortable beds and onto the street. While the gong's shrill sound lingered, a few patrons appeared, still disheveled and red-eyed. Alternately yawning and muttering incoherent prayers, they dropped rice packages into the monks' bowls.

But the gong evidently served another purpose as well. I had read somewhere, or heard someone say, that Napoleon Bonaparte could sleep with his eyes open while riding a horse. It was, perhaps, a form of sleepwalking. In other words, he could sleep-ride. And now I saw with my own eyes Buddhist monks who were sleep-marching; they moved along in synchronized steps with the wakeful ones, but their heads were tilted to the side, and their eyes closed, each in an expression of serenity that could have only come from an inactive mind. It was also for these sleep-marchers' benefit that the gong sang; I saw them jerked back into consciousness each time the venerable instrument was struck. The music of the gong was Buddha's calling, to which both his benefactors and disciples must answer.

In some parts of the neighborhood, I saw newly erected apartment complexes sharing the sidewalks with clusters of hovels and huts. Like over-grown bullies among malnourished youths, the wide-shouldered brick buildings intimidated their tiny, misshapen neighbors. But before each home—be it a spacious teak mansion encircled with fragrant rosebushes or a collapsing bamboo structure with a crude, thatched roof—was a ditch filled with foul, dark liquid. Partially covered with broken concrete plates, some of these ditches resembled gaping mouths with broken teeth. Those that were simply left exposed, on the other hand, looked like moats, whose sole purpose was to drown an invading army.

These ditches, in actuality, are part of the city's sewage system; whereas San Francisco and New York choose to confine their drainage, for the most part, to underground tunnels and channels, Rangoon, with unabashed candor, reveals its intestinal functions to curious onlookers, just as a master clockmaker might, out of professional pride, showcase the intricate mechanism of his latest creation. During monsoon months, when streams and creeks overflow, fishes and shrimps can be seen jumping in and out of Rangoon's sewers; it is not uncommon to see an urban angler (usually a boy in a plastic raincoat with a broken branch, a line, and a wiggling worm impaled on a safety pin) poised above a sewer, ready to reel in his dinner.

Growing up, I saw a wide variety of sewers, but I couldn't recall seeing any as deep and as menacing as those in Tamwe. The only good thing I can say about them is that they are too big to miss, and since the dark matters underneath the water emit a kind of phosphorescent glow, they are impossible to miss—and that makes them safe. But danger came with a sudden power outage, and all the street lamps died instantly, leaving me with the dreadful knowledge that I was surrounded by sewers, each of which could easily devour a small army.

I had heard the incredible story—an urban legend of sorts—of a local man who went out for a walk with his wife one morning and didn't realize she had fallen into a ditch until he got home. There were several versions of the story but in all the versions I had heard, the wife was eventually found dead. I imagined myself at the bottom of a sewer, unrecognizable except for my yellow-and-maroon tie. The produce merchant would testify: "That was the foreigner I saw going to the market earlier." The cab driver would corroborate: "Yes, that's him." The older monks would say a few prayers for my soul.

The younger ones, for whom the only lesson was that it looked extremely ridiculous to lie at the bottom of a sewer with a tie, would laugh hysterically and move on. I would never get to see Kandawgyi. Farewell Rangoon!

Power outages are an accepted part of life in Burma. I remember them occurring with the regularity of lunar cycles when I was growing up. My mother knew exactly when to bring out the candles, and I knew exactly when I would get to play with melting wax. If our section of the street was without electricity this Thursday, then next Thursday would be our next-door neighbors' turn. That was how the government conserved electricity. However, this equilibrium of light and dark was sometimes thrown into disarray by the terrorist attacks of tribal rebels struggling for autonomy and independence from the oppressive military regime. Once in a while, these rebel factions bombed power plants to make a political statement. When this happened, the entire city could be in the dark for weeks.

I did get to see Kandawgyi later. It seemed Tamwe was fully prepared for the power outage; as soon as the street lamps went out, candles and gas lamps began to illuminate the entire neighborhood. I found Bagan Inn, my temporary residence, fully lit when I returned. Evidently the prudent owner of the establishment had invested in a power generator. "We were sort of expecting this," said the receptionist. Was he informed in advance that there would be a power outage? "No, we know it's our turn this week because that section over there lost power last week." Apparently, the same energy conservation plan was still in place.

The power returned a few hours later. By then, sunlight was pouring in through the bamboo screens of my windows. Having survived the power outage and the sewers unscathed, I felt invincible. So I went out, for the second time, to look for Kandawgyi. This time, I didn't bother asking for directions. There were only two possible turns and I had already taken the wrong one earlier. Therefore, I reasoned, the one I had failed to take previously had to be the right one. When I reached the same intersection, without any hesitation whatsoever, I turned left. Eventually, I found Kandawgyi.

When I walked past a family of four, the two children—a boy and a girl in matching outfits—said, "Look, a foreigner!" I had always had unusually pale skin. The harsh Asian sun failed to bronze me properly during the years in my childhood. The mild northern Californian sun did little to my skin tone. I had distinct Chinese features, framed within a mustache and a beard I had grown to hide my boyishness. But most importantly, I had a necktie—the unmistakable trademark of a foreigner.

"Don't stare," said the father, who was flapping his arms as if he were a plane getting ready to take off. "It's impolite." His—as incredible as it was—was not the most unique form of exercise; there were many others who, facing the magnificent Shwe Dagon pagoda, rotated their limbs in such unnatural fashions that I was tempted to conclude they were either testing the durability of their joints or practicing to become contortionists. I too used to jog around Kandawgyi. My motivation, however, was not personal fitness but vanity.

When I was sixteen, I received a pair of Nike shoes—something not many adolescent boys in Burma could afford. It was a present from a relative who had migrated to Canada. It arrived, like a sacred object from heaven, in a shiny cardboard box with a curved arrow on the lid. The unveiling ceremony was attended by many of my playfellows. When the crumpled tissues were removed and the shoes brought out, everyone had something to say about them. *Look at the size of it! Have you ever seen anything that big? I have seen a pair exactly like this, worn by such and such actor in such and such movie. Yes, but did you see a similar pair worn by such and such singer during his concert tour? How much do you think it'll cost in Bogyoke Market?*

At the time, in Bogyoke Market, a pair of Nike shoes was sold for three or four times the salary of a low-level government official. It was not just a pair of running shoes—it was a piece of the Free West—the opulent land of *Dallas* and *Dynasty*, accessible to most Burmese only through television sets and movie screens. My new Nikes, upon closer examination, revealed the label "Made in Taiwan," but because it was Nike, it was still a symbolic representation of the West, just as Marlboro and Ray-Ban had always been, regardless of where they were actually manufactured. Being the proud owner, I had to find an excuse to showcase my new shoes; I began waking up at five—a thing I had never done in the past—to jog around Kandawgyi. When I stretched, to let everyone know I was wearing Nike shoes, I kicked the air with impunity (something nearly impossible to execute with finesse wearing traditional Burmese thongs). The curved arrows on my shoes shone in the sun like thunderbolts from the Olympian goddess of victory.

Shwe Dagon, the legendary pagoda, stood at a distance like a golden lotus rising to meet the sky. Karaweik Hotel, which was built in the style of a royal barge, serenely rested on the water. The two mythical birds shouldering the hotel threw the massive shadows of their beaks across the water. The hotel was anchored, but the water was flowing. It gave the illusion that the hotel was moving too. With fancy hotels rising from the ground every day and flashy cars whizzing by every second, the Rangoon that I saw on my return also appeared to be moving in fast forward. But that too was an illusion. Eventually, I found out that a decent sarong cost half the salary of an average government clerk, a bag of rice the entire salary of the clerk, and a pair of imported sneakers still four times the salary of the clerk's boss. The city had hardly moved in the past ten years.

When the father realized that his children were still staring at me, he slapped the back of their heads with considerable force. Then, he and his wife began staring at me. "Looks like a Malaysian," he remarked. "Could be a Japanese," she observed. And the two proceeded to discuss my attire. *Look at that flashy tie! Do you see that tie? Who wears a tie that early in the morning on such a hot day? Silly, isn't it? But it's a good tie though. I might wear it, but only if I were going to wedding or a dinner party. And the shoes! Look at those shoes!*

I read voraciously when I was growing up. Years of living abroad might have dulled my Burmese grammar and spelling, but I could still efficiently speak my native language. So I understood everything they were saying. But I pretended not to. I had pledged allegiance to the American flag. I was carrying an American passport. I was—legally—an American, a foreigner. It was their right to treat me as one.

And it was also my right to act like one. I used to look at foreigners the way they did—with a mixture of contempt and jealousy. My parents used to take me to Maha Bandoola Park, which was a couple of blocks away from the Strand Hotel, an establishment well-known for its colonial charm and a favorite among British tourists. Seen against the backdrop of discolored, gray buildings, the whitewashed hotel from the 1900s, with uniformed attendants beneath its brightly lit colonnade, was an enviable sight. I observed the foreigners coming and going. I marveled at the ease with which they climbed in and out of the moving iron-box (the elevator). These pink-skinned, sandy-haired creatures, whose body scent was not of sweat and shame like mine, but of powder and brandy, intimidated me with their self-assured, self-possessed demeanors. They roared; we whimpered. They strode in pride; we cowered in fear. Watching them from the opposite sidewalk, I felt a great despair, for I knew they had seen and done things I could only dream of. And I had prayed fervently to become a foreigner some day.

Being a foreigner in my own native country added yet another dimension to the kaleidoscopic vision that was my self. The necktie I had chosen to wear that morning was both ennobling and stifling. I insisted on wearing it because I recognized the prestige it suggested. I was a foreigner and, at the same time, a native coming home. One identity offered me a sense of belonging and the other alien-ation. Ironically, it was my foreigner identity, which came with a tourist's remorselessness, that made me feel as if I belonged in Burma as much as I did anywhere else, and it was my identity as a home-coming native, which implied that I had at one point chosen to forsake my motherland, that made me feel alienated. So I behaved like a foreigner, while wishing everyone I met would somehow recognize me as a returning native. But that was ridiculous as I was doing everything I could to make the locals think that I was a foreigner and nothing to reveal that I was once a native.

Preoccupied, I detoured through another neigh-borhood on my way back to the inn. I went through a labyrinth of short lanes with multiple exits, and when I came out on the other side, I was on an unfa-miliar road. There was a sidewalk tea shop, operating underneath a tarpaulin sheet stretched and mounted on four bamboo poles. There were a few *side-cars* (tricycles with passenger seats attached on the side) parked outside. The *side-car sayas* (side-car operators) temporarily deserted a tic-tac-toe match in progress, where the two players used broken branches to draw their *X*s and *O*s in the sand, to observe what I—the lost foreigner—would do next. Those in the tea shop also began to turn around, one by one, to observe me. One of the *side-car sayas* cried, "Sir, where you want to go?" A sensible foreigner would have ridden the *side-car* back to the inn for an agreeable fee. But I was leaden with guilt and shame, and I felt embarrassed to admit to them, and to myself, that I was lost. I had no excuse to be lost—I was a home-coming native. I walked a few blocks away from the tea shop and approached instead a young girl selling flowers at an intersection.

In casual conversations, the Burmese tend to address strangers as if they are relations; when I was growing up, both my upstairs neighbor and my next-door neighbor (the former an unmarried Indian doctor, and the latter a monkish Burmese bachelor) called me *thar* (son). I did some rough calculations in my head, and concluded that, if I were married, my daughter would be the same age as this flower girl. So I decided to call her *thami* (daughter).

"*Thami*," I asked, "how do I get back to Bagan Inn on Po Sein Street?" She looked at me in astonishment. I was in appearance a foreigner through and through, yet I was speaking to her in unaccented Burmese; that was something new to her. I could imagine the dinner-table conversation at her house that night: *Mom, Dad, let me tell you about this Singaporean man that I met this morning—he spoke to me in Burmese!* My second "*thami*" didn't accomplish anything, but my third "*thami*," reinforced by a light tap on her shoulder, finally brought her out of her stupefied state.

"Would you like to buy some flowers?" asked my enterprising *thami*, handing me a string of gardenias whose petals were already turning brown from exposure to heat and dust. I gave her 100 kyats and told her to keep the change. The prevailing exchange rate at the time was 340 kyats for a dollar; the amount I gave her was less than 30 cents. But what I gave her was probably more than what she normally made in her entire day.

"You can take a shortcut through that hospital over there," she said, pointing at a mossy structure behind an iron gate. The sign above the gate read "Workers' Hospital." "Go through the hospital compound. Take the passage on the side and go through the *khwe-toe-bouk*." The term means "dog hole." The road to the inn, I was assured by my *thami*, was on the other side of this dog hole.

I entered, following a group of uniformed nurses coming to work. I followed closely behind them as they entered from the main entrance. They were giggling and teasing one another at first, but when they saw me head for the dog hole, they all became alarmed. I overheard their whispers. *A lost tourist, I think. Does he know where he's going? Doesn't look like it. Shall we stop him? Quick, someone go talk to him! You go! No, you go!* I was drenched in sweat and I was hungry. I wanted, more than anything, to be back in my air-conditioned room, having breakfast. So I dismissed their whispers and kept walking. The path stretched behind a series of one-story structures with rustic plumbing. At the end of the path, I found half a dozen starving street dogs, nosing through the putrid content of a dumping ground in search of breakfast, their ribcages visibly trembling underneath their brown skins. Beyond them, I saw a large gate that was closed, and a side door that was open. The door—if it *was* to be regarded as such—was a metal plate attached to a rustic frame about the size of a small stove. And I became certain I had found the shortcut I was looking for when I saw one of the street dogs squeeze itself through the tiny gap underneath the frame—this was the *khwe-toe-bouk* my *thami* had directed me to.

I am not a big man by any means; I stand only five feet six inches, and I have what could be categorized as a medium build. But I was not going to be able to walk through this dog hole with my head held high. In order to go through it, I would need to adopt an involuntary posture of humility, bend down, and crawl through it, right behind the other dogs. This was a devastating blow to my dignity, but I had no choice: I had a few minutes to get back to the inn before breakfast was served, so I began my laborious exit. And that was when I noticed a series of blocky Burmese characters painted on the wall. *Warning: Morgue—Corpses Kept Here.* I suddenly understood why there was no one around and why the nurses looked alarmed earlier.

I had a superstitious friend who was terrified of black cats. "The ones that have some colored patches here and there—they're all right," he once stated his theory, "but the ones that are completely black— they are evil. You'd better stay away from them." He refused to walk along the path such a black cat had walked across. To him, they were signs of impending doom. If he had learned that within the first few hours of my arrival, I had had a vision of myself at the bottom of a sewer and I had literally walked through a *khwe-toe-bouk* behind a morgue, he would probably say, "These are signs—they're trying to tell you something." But what were they telling me?

They were probably mother Burma's way of saying, "You are no longer in the safe bosom of your foster father." They were her gentle, and not so gentle, reminders that I was back in her house, where darkness, disillusion, and death were all parts of daily life. In the hours following breakfast, I sat on my bed in my room and listened to the voices of the city—the muddled incantations of drowsy monks returning to the monastery, their despondent gong, the gut-wrenching squeal (*"Pe byuuoooooke!"*) of a pavement-treading baked-bean seller with a heavy wicker basket on her head. They all sounded reproachful and rapturous—a curious mixture of euphoria and despair—like the choking words of an ambivalent mother who was still unsure whether she should kiss or slap her homecoming son.

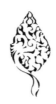

The Colonial Tongue

When I was growing up in Rangoon, there were two official English papers (*The Guardian* and *Working People's Daily*), both scrupulously censored by the government. The existence of two newspapers with different names gave one the deceptive notion that there was a choice, but it was in actuality a choice between two identical twins, both of whom were inflicted with severe pathological dishonesty, so the choice hardly mattered. Both papers ran the same stories in not too many different words—same editorials, same headlines, same obituaries. A typical story would be about a government minister, who was invariably an army officer of considerable distinction, on an inspection tour. On average, two to three of these stories were reported each day; and on days when there was a serious shortage of news, the same general was featured in all three stories. Recently, I discovered through Burmese government's official Web site (www.myanmar.com) that a Burmese paper that had been around for quite some time was now available in English, under the name *The New Light of Myanmar* (www.myanmar.com/

nlm/). Perusing some of its pages posted on the site, I discovered that it too featured stories of army officers on inspection tours:

> Minister Inspects Kalewa Coal Mine
>
> YANGON, 30 Nov—Minister for Mines Brig-Gen Ohn Myint inspected Kalewa coal mine of No 3 Mining Enterprise . . . .
>
> Accompanied by officials, the minister heard a report on target production of the mine and finding of the coal deposits with the use of drilling machines. After giving suggestions to officials, the minister inspected . . . .
>
> Secretary-2 Inspects Poultry Farm in Mingaladon
>
> YANGON, 12 Dec—Secretary-2 of the State Peace and Development Council Lt-Gen Tin Oo, accompanied by Minister for Commerce, . . . inspected the poultry farm of Yangon City Development Committee . . . .
>
> The Secretary-2 then left necessary instructions.

On December 13, according to headlines in *The New Light of Myanmar*, while Lt. General Tin Oo was on his way from a sugar mill in Pyay to a cotton mill in Taungdwingyi, his colleague Maj. General Hla Myint Shwe, Minister of Transport, was inspecting the new extension of Putao Airport. And finding "the apron, runways, fencing of the airport and the signboard at the end of the runway" satisfactory, the Transport Minister went on to inspect a suspension bridge in the nearby Mulashidi Village. Both the Commerce Minister and the Transport Minister, I'm sure, gave a few unsolicited instructions before departing.

During my trip to Rangoon, I returned to the curbside tea shop that I used to visit regularly in my adolescence. The proprietor—a loud, impassioned Pakistani man with a great repertoire of satirical political anecdotes—approached me. He was reluctant at first, but once he recognized me, he immediately abandoned the tea shop's operations to his assistant—his teenage son—and invited himself to my table for a cup of his own tea. Perhaps he could, I suggested, entertain me with a story. He obliged readily.

When a Burmese general recently visited a shipyard, began my storyteller, the following exchange took place.

"Why hasn't this ship been put to sea yet?" asked the general, who was surrounded by a number of nervous civilian authorities, when he noticed a ship that was sitting idle by the dock.

"We need some mechanical parts that are not available domestically," explained one of the engineers standing nearby, "and if we order them from abroad, the construction cost will exceed our budget."

"Well, what are those parts?" demanded the general. The engineer listed the parts. Since there were no equivalent terms to describe these mechanical items in Burmese, they were named—necessarily—in English.

"I don't care," screamed the general. "Whatever they are, just order them, get them here, and finish the job!"

Then he noticed another ship that was sitting idle and the question was again raised: "What about this one over there?" The engineer once again recited a list of foreign-made mechanisms required to complete the ship, and the general once again told him to "just order them!" By the time he discovered the third idle ship, the general was so furious he began employing every conceivable epithet in his speech. (And my storyteller, eager for verisimilitude, also employed at this point a wide variety of vulgarities, savoring every single one as he pronounced them.)

"I suppose this one needs some foreign parts too," the general said sarcastically.

"This one, general, " answered the engineer with an embarrassed smile, "can be put to sea immediately, if it weren't for bad *weather*."

His reply was in Burmese, with the exception of the word *weather*. But the general, who presumably had no English education and no idea what *weather* meant, said, "Then, by all means, order a new *weather!*"

There were times during my visit when I wished I could order a different weather—a milder, cooler one with temperatures in the low 70s. Any movement I made—however strenuous or mild—produced sweat. A visit to the tea shop in the early morning hours—even by cab—left me drenched. After sending my clothes to the inn's housekeeping staff, I was left with two clean shirts to wear. Asian mothers—mother Burma included—know how to make a son feel guilty without resorting to hostility. Finding herself in disagreement with a son, an Asian mother will pour herself a cup of scalding hot tea, and say, "Do whatever makes you happy." But she will, at the same time, let her son see her steamy tears, which burn as much as the tea she pretends to drink. Eventually, it becomes impossible for a son to distinguish his mother's genuine consents from those given unwillingly. And that was the same suspicion with which I viewed Burma's out-of-season heat—I couldn't determine if it was merely an atypical weather phenomenon or my motherland's sulking welcome. Either way, I had traveled half way around the globe to be back in Rangoon, and I was not about to be impeded by anything—neither guilt nor heat.

I was planning to locate an old classmate of mine from Rangoon University from his last known address of a decade ago. Something told me this was going to require numerous lengthy cab rides across town. I knew that I couldn't possibly order a different weather. So I ordered the next best thing— an air-conditioned cab.

"Recession," answered the young lady at the front desk when I rang. It took me a while to figure out what she meant. Finding the verbal transition from p to t too difficult to manage, she dropped the first of the two intermediary consonants, turning *reception* into *recession*. I asked her to find me an air-conditioned cab. When I gave the driver my friend's address, he scratched his head and asked, "What's the new name for this road?" The young lady looked at the address, which read Lewis Road, and replied, "I think it's now called Seik Kan Tha Road (Scenic Harbor Road)." The gardener and the cook also came over and examined my friend's decade-old address. After holding a brief conference, they all came to an agreement—my destination was Seik Kan Tha Road.

Years ago, in its attempt to nurse the dying national language back to life, the Burmese govern-ment began an unofficial anti-English campaign. Prominent government officials began making carefully worded speeches, in which they hinted that the usage of English—the language of Burma's former colonial master—was to be discontinued. *The Guardian* and *Working People's Daily* printed those speeches, verbatim. The message was heard loud and clear: It was time to expel the lingering ghost of the British Empire. One Monday morning, our Burmese teacher walked into the classroom and gave us a speech of her own on the merits of the national language. Burma, she argued, was independent now, so there was no need to study English. "It's about time," she cried excitedly, "we do away with this horrid colonial language." We were excited too, but for a different reason—she was too wrapped up in her own newfound patriotism that she forgot to give us homework.

In 1989, like an overeager surgeon performing an unnecessary amputation on a patient or an ill-advised exorcist sprinkling holy water on bystanders, the Burmese government replaced all the English names of cities, townships, and streets with Burmese names, and officially changed the country's name from Burma to Myanmar and the country capital's name from Rangoon to Yangon. Hence the transformation from Lewis Road to Seik Kan Tha Road. At schools and colleges, there was a steady decline in English education. By the time the Ministry of Education recognized the folly of this campaign and quietly adopted a friendlier policy towards English, irreparable damage had already been done. "Recession" was just one of the many effects.

Cabs in Rangoon do not operate on mileage. In fact, they rarely have odometers that are in operation. One has to bargain with them before getting in.

"How much?" I asked the cab driver.

"Will I have to turn on the air-conditioner?" he asked.

I said he would—after all, that was the reason I had specifically asked for an air-conditioned cab. "Then it'll be 350 kyats," he said. I offered 250 kyats. "Well, I'll take you there," he said, "but you won't get air-conditioning at that price." He had apparently discovered my weakness. We agreed on 300 kyats, with air-conditioning. I settled into the back seat and we took off, with all the windows rolled up, listening to Shania Twain singing, "That don't impress me much."

Fifteen minutes into the ride, I noticed I couldn't feel the air-conditioner, and the car was traveling a bit too slowly. The interior of the cab was as hot as that of a steam engine. I waited five more minutes. Still, there was no improvement in my comfort level, so I began thinking I should just roll down the windows and let in the wind. Noticing the way I was fidgeting, the driver turned around and apologetically said, "Sometimes the air-conditioner dies when I speed up or play the stereo too loud." But how could these seemingly unrelated operations affect one another? "Because," he explained, "the air-conditioner, the stereo, and the engine all share the same battery." I was no mechanic, so I had no way to dispute his claim. I told him to shut the air-conditioner off, shut Shania Twain up, and speed up. "But we have already agreed on 300 kyats," he reminded me, looking disappointed. I told him I would pay 300 kyats regardless.

Downtown introduced itself to me like the aging headmistress of my old high school. I had never been able to make up my mind about her. I remembered her being much taller and statelier, but she now stood feebly before me—decrepit, pale, and reeking of cigarette smoke. At Sule Pagoda Circle, where traffic used to flow freely, I saw cars coming to a halt. Drivers coughed up and spat out profanities from their throbbing jugular veins. This was the clog in Rangoon's arteries; if no civil engineering team would perform a bypass surgery soon, the traffic would eventually kill the city.

The new additions to the district were easy to spot, for the bright young buildings shunned the older neighbors with whom they were forced to share the sidewalk; the sporadic patches of bright colors on mossy, gray walls made downtown look like an old matron in an ill-suited psychedelic outfit. Not that Rangoon's downtown had decayed that much, that fast, but I had seen many healthier, livelier downtown districts; so the neoclassical colonnades, the triangular pediments, the round-arch windows, the cornices, the verandas, and the balustrades—however stately and majestic these colonial architectural splendors might have been in the 1940s when Clement Atlee was Britain's prime minister—now looked undeniably dated and antiquated, better suited for museum exhibitions and curio shops. And, like an old principal who knew she couldn't survive on pension alone, Rangoon refused to retire and insisted on receiving visitors, some of whom shrank when they were confronted by the city's spectral façade for the first time. Love her or hate her, she was *my* old headmistress and I was only too glad to see her.

When we arrived at Seik Kan Tha Road (which was neither scenic nor anywhere near a harbor) I asked the cab driver to park and wait. It wasn't too difficult to find the apartment building, since it still stood exactly where it did when I had visited my friend more than ten years ago. The rain-washed panels on the verandas were still mossy and discolored, and the cavernous cracks in the plaster were still agape. I climbed four flights of stairs, lit dimly by the sunlight peeping through barred windows located near landings between flights. When I knocked on the door, a frightened child stared at me through a large keyhole. I mentioned my friend's name, and I was instructed to go up one more flight. I did, and knocked again, only to be greeted by a disheveled lady, whose siesta I had obviously interrupted.

"You're looking for Soe Myint," she asked, "from the English Department of Rangoon University?" I said I was. "The short, stout one with really dark skin?" she asked again, to confirm. I conceded that my friend could be described in such a fashion. "Well, he doesn't live here anymore," she said, "but you should go to his brother's house," and she scribbled on a piece of paper my new destination. That was encouraging, I thought, because I didn't expect a new tenant to be able to provide such detailed information about a previous tenant. "It's because I'm his sister," she later explained. I asked if there was a specific hour of the day during which my friend was most likely to be found at this new address—noon, night, or midnight? "Well," she replied, "you might not find him there at all, but his brother will be able to tell you where he is." I thanked her, and climbed five flights down. Still trying to catch my breath, I gave the cab driver my new destination. It was on Yogi Road (Mystic Road). The ride would now take me back in the direction that I had just come from. He offered to take me there for 300 kyats more. I accepted, stipulating that both the air-conditioner and the stereo would remain off.

My cab driver, as it turned out, was well-read and thoroughly knowledgeable on Burmese novels, classic and contemporary. So I was fairly compensated for my lack of comfort with a lively literary discussion. He was, as I had once been, a fan of the Burmese novelist Min Thein Kha, who authored a series of murder mysteries featuring two members of the Imperial Police Force from colonial days. Min Thein Kha's hero Hnin Maung, just like Conan Doyle's Holmes, was an excellent violinist and a skilled amateur boxer. He was also a master of the science of deduction; he could reconstruct a murder scene from seemingly insignificant clues such as a match or a strand of hair. His friend Aung Thin, just like Watson, was benevolent but naïve and somewhat dimwitted. Together, those two Burmese patriots begrudgingly served the British bureaucrats, pursuing—often against their will—villains who were mostly righteous nationalists wronged by the colonial judicial system.

Eventually, I began reading Doyle in English and discovered that Min Thein Kha was plagiarizing. I would not have accused him of plagiarism for the sheer similarities between his characters and those of Doyle. In this respect, he was no more a plagiarist than Doyle; Doyle's Holmes was nothing but the Edwardian version of Poe's Auguste Dupin. What troubled me, more than the obvious parallels between his earlier works and those of Doyle, was his utter failure to acknowledge Doyle. There was a perfunctory reference to Doyle in his novel *Hnin Maung and Three Bees (Sar Pulin Hnin Maung hnit Bedone Thone Gong)*, but it was not Min Thein Kha who mentioned Doyle—it was Dagon Shwe Mya, another respected Burmese novelist who provided an introduction to the novel. And in another novel of his, called *Hnin Maung and the Mystery Shrouded from Head to Toe (Sar Pulin Hnin Maung hnit Gong Myi Chone Lone Ba Pe)*, Min Thein Kha, with characteristic Buddhist humility, expressed his indebtedness to his two literary mentors:

I, with my forehead touching the ground, pay homage to my two masters—Dagon Shwe Mya (Golden Arrow of Dagon) and Shwe U Dong (Golden Peacock)—whose solid styles and plot-structures I have been imitating as closely as possible.

For the truth of this statement, may my writing endure as long as theirs do.

Those two masters, whose styles and plots he had been imitating, were themselves translators of Sherlock Holmes mysteries. The two novels of his mentioned above were Doyle's *A Study in Scarlet* and *The Valley of Fear*, translated almost word for word and embellished with Burmese myths and legends. Why he would, with such reverence, pay homage to the two translators but fail to do the same to Doyle, was the mystery I had once tried to solve. Holmes' famous science of deduction may or may not be of any help here, but an understanding of the Burmese nationalistic attitude might. I could think of two possible explanations for Min Thein

Kha's behavior. One: Because he borrowed from the works of the translators and not directly from the originals, he felt he was not indebted to the original author. This, as scandalous as it may seem in the West, is an unchallenged practice among the Burmese literati. Two: He was too embarrassed to admit that he was indebted to an English author. Wasn't it enough that his two native heroes had to suffer every form of indignity like all sepoys while serving their colonial masters? Would he, the author, also have to pay tribute to Doyle? This was just too much. He would much rather be a plagiarist than admit that his muse was a mustached, portly English man. Ironically, or perhaps understandably, this was quite similar to the attitude of the villains in his stories: they would rather become fugitives than serve under the yolk of the British empire.

In all fairness, it must be stated that his later works, such as *Hnin Maung and the Demon of Myaing Yaza (Sar Pulin Hnin Maung hnit Myaing Yaza Tarte)* or *Saturday Maung Maung (Sanay Maung Maung)*, bore little or no relation to any of Doyle's works. In this respect, he was similar to an art student who began by copying the works of the ancient masters; eventually, he matured and found his own style. The students my uncle encountered while teaching English at Rangoon University, on the other hand, were a different breed of plagiarists.

"Every year, they came to me with the same graduation paper," said my uncle, wiping his glasses and shaking his head helplessly. "Everyone turned in *The Origin of the English Novel*, which was any-thing but original; I had seen the same thesis and the same argument so many times I could even recite it by heart." Couldn't he simply give these papers failing grades? "That would be eighty percent of them," he said, repeating it with emphasis: "Eighty percent!" Could he perhaps ask these students to rewrite their papers? "Well, I could ask them to rewrite the papers, but I couldn't possibly demand originality from them; some of them obviously couldn't even construct a decent sentence without help." So what was his compromise? "I suggested that if they find it necessary to steal, at least they try to steal from *several* different sources so it's not too obvious."

Even in the 1980s, when I was still attending classes at Rangoon University, the effect of the anti-English campaign was already widespread. Beside those who had worked for foreign companies or those who had attended missionary schools, very few could read, write, or speak English in an acceptable manner.

We—the English major students—were the shameless few who dared to study the disgraced language. We read plays by Shakespeare and Shaw and poems by Wordsworth and Longfellow. We wrote not only our own papers but those of many others as well. Whenever there was an English paper due (not every paper was required to be written in English), we became the most popular group on campus. We had a steady supply of coffee and tea free of charge. We found strangers offering to pay our bills in the canteen. We received invitations from pretty girls who had never acknowledged our overtures in the past. All we had to do was write their papers. So we did—*The Three Main Causes of the First Anglo-Burmese War* for the poor chaps from the History Department, and *Common Logical Fallacies* for the dimpled darlings from the Philosophy Department, and many more for many others.

In the past four or five years, foreign investors began arriving in Burma. Hotel Nikko stood at the corner of Po Sein Street and Nat Mauk Road, monopolizing the best possible view of Kandawgyi and Shwe Dagon. Traders Hotel stood where Pa Pa Win Cinema once did, establishing itself at the center of downtown Rangoon. Ramada greeted the tourists upon arrival, standing right next to Mingaladon Airport of Rangoon. And Daewoo set up office on Yaw Min Gyi Road in Dagon Township. The language that had been suppressed became absolutely essential to the economic success of the country. The officials, who had to regularly interact with foreign investors, were now forced to take English lessons. The affluent sought English tutors for their sons and daughters. Employers sought English-speaking applicants. Once again, those who were fluent in English found themselves highly in demand. Ironically, the English-educated benefited more than the others did from this anti-English campaign.

After retiring from his job as a lecturer, my uncle began giving private lessons. He managed three or four *tables* a year. (Local people use the term *table* for an assembly of five to ten students who meet at a specific location once or twice a week to receive private lessons on a chosen subject.) Now retired, my uncle raced from *table* to *table*, in a manner of speaking, giving private English lessons from morning to noon every day. What he made in his retirement was ten times the salary he made at Rangoon University.

I had previously been informed in a letter that Soe Myint, the friend I was trying to locate, was working as a tutor in the English Department of Rangoon University. So, on a plane somewhere over the Pacific Ocean, watching Richard Gere and Julia Roberts meet for the first time in *Runaway Bride* on a flickering screen, I conceived an idea—a master plan—to make our reunion much more dramatic than it would ordinarily be if it were left to chance. I would find out his class schedule, and I would attend his class. Just as he was finishing his lecture, he would ask his students if they had any questions. And that was exactly the moment I would make my presence known. I would raise my hand, and ask him a series of silly questions. I knew not what they were at the time, but I was fairly confident I could come up with a few that involved Hamlet: *Excuse me sir, but when he said, "Ay, there's the rub!" could he possibly be talking about . . .?* Oh, what a moment that would be!

After a long conversation on Min Thein Kha and Conan Doyle, the cab pulled up in front of a modest wooden house on Yogi Road where my friend's brother supposedly lived. I went in and introduced myself to a man who looked like a younger version of my friend. I stated the purpose of my visit. "My brother occasionally comes here, but he doesn't live here," he said. So where did my friend Soe Myint live? Surely he lived somewhere. "He lives on campus, at Raminya Hall, where the teaching staff lives." I thanked him, and got up to return to my cab. "But you won't find him there either." I stopped again. "See, our mother is ill, so he has been sleeping over at Bahosi Medical Center." Then I was provided with the address of the hospital and the room number where my friend's mother was. The young cab driver, as before, offered to take me there for 300 kyats additional.

I arrived just before noon. Passing a tea shop on my way to the main gate, I heard whispers behind me. *Think he's a doctor? Couldn't be from here; we've never seen him before. Maybe a specialist who's just flown from Japan. What's he doing here? Where's his briefcase and stethoscope?* I walked up to a glass booth, inside which stood two uniformed nurses. I mentioned the room number to them. Up to this point, I had been speaking with everyone—the cab driver, my friend's sister, and my friend's brother—in Burmese, but when I approached the nurses, I instinctively began speaking English. The effect was almost immediate.

"Foreigner," whispered one nurse to the other. Before my arrival, she had been processing a long line of incoming patients. From the way they pressed various parts of their bodies and groaned, I could tell many of them needed immediate medical attention. Yet she came out of the booth to personally escort me to the elevator. Not only did she ride the elevator with me but she also walked me down the corridor and led me straight to the room I sought. I wasn't sure she would have accorded me the same attentiveness if I hadn't worn a tie or spoken English.

A foreigner is something of an exotic creature in Burma, which is why the natives sometimes give him preferential treatment. I felt awkward receiving this treatment because I knew she temporarily neglected those who deserved her attention more than I did. I had previously thought that, being both a foreigner and a native, I could choose when I wanted be a foreigner and when a native. But I was beginning to realize that the natives assumed what I was quicker than I could declare what I wanted to be. And once they had made the assumption that I was a foreigner, I had no choice but to go along; revealing that I was a native after they had treated me like a foreigner would be an embarrassment not just to myself but also to them.

I saw an elderly lady lying on a bed, surrounded by a score of visitors, some sitting, and some standing. From behind, without seeing their faces, I couldn't identify my friend, because all the men in the room were of the same height and built. So I called out his name, and waited for someone to turn around.

Soe Myint!

Everyone turned around. A dozen pairs of eyes examined me in confusion. Among the faces, I recognized one that was the face of my friend Soe Myint. It took him longer to recognize me, but when he finally did, the confusion on his face turned to disbelief, and a smile emerged from the corner of his lips. We shook hands for the first time in a decade. He, as he used to, greeted me in English, and I, without thinking twice, responded in English. To us, English was not a colonial language; it was merely a language that we both understood and felt comfortable speaking. Oh, what a moment that was!

A month before my trip, when I telephoned the Burmese Embassy in Washington D.C. to get my visa, the following exchange took place.

"Have you been back to *Yangon* recently?"

"I left *Rangoon* ten years ago, and I haven't been back since."

"Then you'll need to fill out a biography form."

"You'll send it to my home?"

"Yes."

The form turned out to be eleven-pages long, with questions on both sides, asking me everything from where I used to live to what my religion was.

"Have a nice stay in *Myanmar*."

"Thank you—I am looking forward to visit *Burma* again."

The embassy staff politely insisted, as diplomats are trained to do, on the new names—*Yangon* instead of *Rangoon*, *Myanmar* instead of *Burma*. And I kept referring to the country and the city by their former names. In the biography form, I wrote down my birthplace as *Rangoon*. It was a linguistic tug of war. But I was not deliberately combating the new names. It was just habit. I had known this country as *Burma* and this city as *Rangoon* since my birth. It was too late for me to change.

Whenever I address my letters to *Yangon, Myanmar*, the postal clerks in San Francisco ask, "Where in the world is *Yangon, Myanmar*?" I rarely have to tell them where in the world *Rangoon, Burma* is—they know. In a way, it is too late for the country too. No general can order a new name for a country any more than he can a different *weather*.

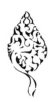

The Guardians
of the Pagoda

The sun rose earlier in Asia. At 6:30 A.M. Rangoon was already bathed in a pool of golden sunlight. I pulled the curtains aside to let the light bounce off my pillows. It helped me wake up. Just as I was finishing my breakfast, I was told that my father and my uncle were waiting for me outside. I suddenly remembered that we had planned to visit Shwe Dagon on that day, so I hastily finished my coffee and went out to meet them.

My father flew from San Francisco to Rangoon to reunite with his younger brother—my uncle. During the entire trip, he stayed at his brother's house, the two of them conversing past midnight and into early morning hours every day.

Together, in my uncle's Nissan, the three of us headed for the pagoda. On the way, we had a discussion on whether my father and I should identify ourselves as foreigners or pose as local residents. Foreigners were required to pay a fee of five dollars per person and three dollars per camera at the temple gate. This was one of the few instances in which being a native was preferable to being a foreigner.

We could have easily evaded the fee by pretending to be local residents since we both spoke fluent Burmese and, if questioned, we both had a local address we could provide—my uncle's. I saw this occasion as an opportunity to resolve my foreigner-or-native dilemma. By paying this fee, I reasoned, I would be procuring the official right to behave like a foreigner, free of guilt. So I suggested that we pay the fee. My father agreed, oblivious of my not-so-honorable motivation. He was a devout Buddhist who didn't like to cheat; he wanted to walk through the gate of Nirvana with a clear conscience.

We entered the pagoda barefoot, as was the custom in most holy places in Asia. There were two mythical lions crouching on each side of the entrance, guarding the gate. But these stately lions, each higher than the tallest palm tree in the vicinity, were not half as diligent as the flower sellers lurking behind them; row after row, they stood, forming a gauntlet so tight that not a single soul could escape them without being assaulted. As soon as we walked in, they advanced towards us from both directions, brandishing colorful bouquets.

"*Ah ko* (brother)," cried one, tickling my nose with wet roses, "take these flowers to the altar, and all your wishes will be fulfilled." Our wish at the moment was to find whoever was in charge of collection fees from foreigners so we could pay our dues and proceed. But no such person could be found nearby. My uncle walked down the corridor and found near the end of it a small office with a sign that read Foreign Visitors Enter Here. We walked into the office, decorated with lacquer boxes and woodcarvings, where a middle-aged man and a young woman sat sipping tea from a misshapen tin pot.

"Welcome, welcome," greeted the man, as if he had been waiting for us all along. Then he engaged us in some small talk. *So where're you folks from? California? But born in Rangoon? Imagine that! Visiting or returning? Good! Good!* We were ready to pay but he was not quite ready to collect yet. It seemed he considered it impolite to collect the fee immediately from us; he wanted to make this look like a voluntary contribution. So only when he felt he had sufficiently befriended us did he proceed with the collection. *That'll be five dollars each please—thank you!* My father and I were given stickers to distinguish ourselves as foreigners. We pasted them on our chests.

"What about the camera?" asked my father.

"Is it a big one?" asked the man with a smile.

I showed him the small Canon dangling from my belt. "Oh, that's too small," he said. "We can't possibly charge you for this. Just go right ahead." Both the man and the young woman seemed so congenial that I couldn't imagine them chasing after tourists who refused to pay. They probably wouldn't. They operated on the premise that everyone was fundamentally good; they trusted that everyone would do the right thing, and those who didn't would eventually be punished. That was characteristically Buddhist.

Ten years ago, on the morning before my departure, I came to Shwe Dagon with a group of friends whom I had known since fourth grade. I remember the choking sadness I had felt, believing I was seeing my playfellows for the last time. I honestly didn't care much for the pagoda itself. I had never liked walking on its heat-absorbent marble tiles. It was like walking on hot coals. They released the heat that they had been absorbing right into my naked soles, forcing me to seek relief on scattered carpets and rugs. For me, the customary walk around the central column in a full circle required much ingenuity, for I had to plan my path along carpeted areas, avoiding the white marble floor like a minefield.

So when I reached the top this time, I instinctively began to look for carpets as I used to. There was not one to be found. I began to panic. But my uncle and my father stepped right onto the white floor. My uncle was a local resident and his feet were probably accustomed to the heat, but my father's feet, like mine, had been sealed off and protected in shoes for years since leaving Burma, so they were no longer heat-resistant. I waited to see how they would respond.

"Hey, the floor isn't as hot as it used to be," exclaimed my father.

"Yes," said my uncle, "these are new Japanese tiles. They stay cool even in the afternoon sun."

Aung Moe, my feline-phobic friend who once warned me about black cats, used to come to the pagoda regularly to meditate. He was a devout Buddhist in the uniquely Burmese sense. Having assimilated much of the local legends and myths through time, Burmese Buddhism presently encompasses everything from meditation to occult. It was the darker, shadier elements of Burmese Buddhism that my friend was more attracted to; he dabbled in a number of esoteric arts, such as palmistry, astrology, and even alchemy. From him I learned about the elusive Boe Boe Aung (Elder Aung). Boe Boe Aung is part-wizard and part-yogi. The specific term in Burmese is *waikza*. A *waikza* stands high up near the top of the hierarchy of Burmese wizardry. The term signifies that he has attained such arcane powers as plunging into the ground, turning mercury into gold, and flying through the air.

He is also immune to staff and sword, supposedly. "He is *doke-pe* (staff-proof), *dah-pe* (sword-proof)," said my friend of his *waikza*. I didn't think of asking if the *waikza* had expanded his immunity to cover new weapons that had come into existence since the Iron Age. Twins Luther and Johnny Htoo, members of the Karen tribe who led a small army of guerrillas against the military regime of Burma, were believed to be immune to bullets and land mines. In an attempt to dissuade the Thai forces from shelling their base near the Thai-Burmese border, Luther and Johnny sent ten fighters from their guerrilla army across the border into Thailand and seized a provincial hospital hostage in January 2000. Unfortunately, the ten chosen fighters were not immune to modern weaponry like their leaders; they were all shot and killed by Thai security forces, which stormed the hospital to free the hostages within. Luther and Johnny could not have possibly attained *waikza*-hood; they were Christian fundamentalists, and that alone would have disqualified them from enrolling in any Burmese Buddhist school of sorcery. Their immunity, if anything, might be an unorthodox Christian miracle, of a sort. But the fact that they needed a miracle to stay alive was a tragedy, for these two legendary guerrilla generals were no more than a pair of twelve-year-old boys.

The age of Boe Boe Aung is shrouded in mystery. Some believe he is a hundred years old. Others believe he is a thousand years old. My friend said he was immortal, which made any discussion of his age moot. He also has a habit of making brief appearances during times of civil unrest, as though to remind everyone he is still alive and ready to intervene. The unsubstantiated Bo Bo Aung sightings in Burma probably rival those of Elvis in the West. For some reason, the great Burmese wizard is seen, most of the time, sitting on the wing of a plane. The sixteen hours I endured during my flight from San Francisco to Rangoon was no picnic. But I hadn't done any air travel when I debated the existence of Elder Aung with my friend, so it didn't occur to me to ask why a *waikza*, who could fly unaided by modern aviation, would rather crouch on the wing of a plane than find some other convenient mode of transportation.

I did inquire about his whereabouts. "He might be hiding in the depth of Sagaing Hills," said my friend, "or on a pilgrimage to Mount Popa." One was as unascertainable as the other. "But one day he will return," my friend assured me, "and make this nation far richer than any other—he'll let gemstones fall from heaven like torrents of rain." I looked up, and saw monsoon clouds gathering above us. Lightening flashed repeatedly, tossing bright silver chains across the dark sky, accompanied by the rippling sounds of thunder. The rain of prosperity would come soon, I thought.

One full moon evening, Aung Moe took me to a small shrine between a pair of winged sphinxes, hidden in the shadow of a tall pipal tree, in an

unpopulated corner of the pagoda. "Don't tell anyone about this shrine," he whispered, in a tone of
Masonic secrecy. I examined the shrine visible
behind a short iron-gate. I saw a small brass Buddha
seated on an open lotus inside a boxy shrine. There
was nothing extraordinary about the idol or the
shrine. So what was the reason for his secrecy?
"This was donated to the pagoda by my ancestors,"
he explained, "so we have exclusive right to this
shrine." I was still trying to understand what he
meant by "exclusive" when he reached into his
satchel, from where I had seen him fish out many an
odd object (the astrological chart of an unknown
child inscribed on a palm leaf, a python-fang, a Xerox
copy of the ink-imprint of a celebrated deceased
monk's left hand, and many more that I can no
longer recall). This time, he produced a small key,
with which he proceeded to unlock the gate.

"Guard it for me," he said, handing me the key,
which I accepted with some trepidation. He lit
candles on each side of the shrine. "Return in two
hours," he said. Then, squeezing himself into an area
no larger than a newspaper spread, he sat down
facing the Buddha and began breathing heavily. I
locked the gate behind him and left him to his meditation. When I looked back from a distance, I saw
him in the dark—a glowing figure bathed in gold
and silver underneath candlelight and moonlight.
It made me want to believe in the *waikza*.

My father and my uncle found the replica of the
great Mingun Bell before I could find Aung Moe's
ancestral shrine. The original bell, cast under the reign
of King Bodawpaya, hung in Mingun Village near
Sagaing. The Burmese pilgrims toll bells traditionally

to announce certain good deeds that have been performed. My father and I had no good deeds to declare but we decided to sample the acoustic glory of the bell regardless. We started climbing the steps to the pavilion where the bell hung. But before we reached the top, a young man in a white shirt wearing a badge appeared from nowhere and stopped us.

"I'm sorry," he said apologetically, "but this area is restricted for the moment." We asked for an explanation. "We have some foreign visitors arriving here very soon," he said, speaking under his breath, as though he were divulging a national secret. We didn't press him for more information because he looked like he might face the firing squad if he had revealed more. But could we, we asked him, at least take some pictures from outside? "Please do it quickly," he replied, looking around uneasily.

Not too far from the replica of the bell, we found the replica of the famous reclining Buddha. But when we approached, another young man wearing an official badge once again stopped us. We were told that we could come back later, but for the time being, the area was closed. "It's just that we have some foreign visitors coming today," explained the young man, looking as nervous as the previous one. My father and I looked at our chests. The foreigner stickers were still there. We thought *we* were the foreign visitors. Later we found out that the former Japanese prime minister was visiting the pagoda at the same time we were. Apparently he had exclusive visitation rights to the pagoda just as my friend did to his ancestral shrine. *All foreigners are equal, but some foreigners are more equal than others.*

When we were about to leave, we noticed that we were being followed by a group of children, the oldest of them about eight. The one who appeared to be the leader—a skinny boy cloaked in what appeared to be a large man's dispossessed shirt—walked closely behind us while the others kept their distance. Occasionally, he would wipe his face with the edge of his drooping sleeves. He waited, until we began walking down a long corridor leading to the exit. There, underneath the vaulted chamber of the corridor, he chose to make his plea.

"*Oo lay gyi* (uncle), *Ah ko gyi* (big brother), please give me some money—I'm hungry and I have nothing to eat." He repeated the plea, as if it was a mantra, as he followed us. He was not new to me. He was there ten years ago, and he would probably still be there if I were to return ten years later. He had a different face and a different body, but the plea was always the same. I felt as if I was watching various actors acting out the same tragic role, in a play about the worst form of reincarnation—a nightmarish cycle of death and rebirth that compels one person to be born and reborn, over and over, into the same miserable existence. That, in Buddhist tradition, is *hell*.

Please give me some money—I'm hungry and I have nothing to eat.

Please give me some money—I'm hungry and I have nothing to eat.

Please give me some money—I'm hungry and I have nothing to eat.

Echoed against the low ceiling of the corridor, his repetitions began to multiply. It was as if we were listening to the cries of tens of thousands of starving children. His followers carefully observed from a distance how we would react to their leader. We wanted to give him something, but we also knew that if we did, we would be mobbed by the others, so we couldn't give him anything. Suddenly the white tiles beneath my feet began to burn deep into my soles even though we were walking in the shade. And there was nowhere to run.

I never saw Aung Moe, or his ancestral shrine, again. When I met my other friends the following week, they told me that he—forsaking his prayer beads—took a clerical job in Singapore and relocated there. I asked if anybody knew his address. No one did. It seemed Aung Moe had become as elusive as Elder Aung, and his whereabouts were as unascertainable as that of the *waikza*.

Domes and spires of pavilions, though sizable in themselves, were dwarfish compared to the central column of Shwe Dagon. Steadfast the pagoda rose, like the hands of an ascetic Buddhist in deep prayer, joined together and raised high above his head, reaching for the sky. I looked up, tracing its elegant outline from base to crown, hoping I would get a glimpse of its pinnacle melting into the blinding sunlight pouring down from heaven. The empty blue sky hurt my eyes. Monsoon clouds were nowhere to be found. Everyone was talking about global warming. I heard rumors that the dry season would persist, eventually turning into an interminable draught. That would be bad for the lotuses of Burma.

The Guardians of the Underworld

Several years ago, the Burmese government decided, as part of its plan to expand Rangoon, to relocate the Chinese cemetery where my grandfather was buried. My uncle, just like the surviving families of the others who were buried there, received a notification. It was quite simple—Rangoon needed more space for shopping centers and parking garages, so the late Mr. Chinchu, my grandfather, would have to move out of his eternal resting place to make room for Giordano and Hang-Ten, whose cotton shirts and baggy pants provided the next generation of Burmese teenagers with a new look and a new identity. (In front of the Giordano store in downtown Rangoon hung a three-story-tall monochrome poster of the late James Dean, disdainfully looking down on the livings shopping below.)

The notice promised Mr. Chinchu a new tomb, located somewhere beyond the city's new boundary and reachable by car in 45 minutes or so, if his surviving son was willing to *contribute* the necessary moving expense. If not, he would be incinerated, along with his neighbors who similarly found the government-sponsored relocation plan disagree-able, and his ashes deposited into a communal tomb. My uncle knew how much his father liked privacy, so he paid the expense and had his father moved to the new cemetery. My father and I decided that, while we were in Rangoon, we should find out for ourselves how comfortable my grandfather would be in his new home.

The long road to the cemetery was deadly. The road cut across a moor like a river of hot clay and dirt. Since my father and I had never been to the new cemetery, my uncle agreed to give up his Sunday morning and drive us there. His pickup truck, which I had previously understood to be a ground-transportation vehicle, was airborne most of the time. It flew up and down the wavy road. It flew in and out of huge holes. I was seated at the back. Because he knew I could easily be thrown off the car, my uncle periodically turned around to see if I was still in the back. Clouds of dust rose as high as my nose at every turn. It was noon. The sun was in my eyes. The temperature was at its highest. In order to get to the Chinese cemetery, we had to drive past the Christian cemetery and the Tamil cemetery. By the time we pulled into the Chinese cemetery, I was barely alive. My grandfather, who had made this journey in an urn, was the lucky one.

I stepped off the truck and examined the land. There was hardly any shelter to speak of. There were a few trees here and there but mostly wild grass and bushes. There was a short wire fence to separate the Chinese territory from those of the Christians and the Tamils. This was like a scale model of the city itself, with the Chinese gathered around China Town, and the Pakistanis around Mogul Road. Rangoon, despite its predominantly Buddhist inhabitants who believe in universal love, is a segregated city. Growing up, I heard many a cruel joke featuring a fat Chinese merchant in his oversized boxer shorts, told to my face because I was Chinese. In fourth grade, when my history teacher recounted how the heroic Burmese warriors, outnumbered by the forces of Kublai Khan, were annihilated while defending the Kingdom of Bagan in the battle of Vochan (dated approximately A.D. 1300), my Burmese classmates glared at me menacingly. I was rescued only by my teacher's timely explanation of the difference between a Mongol and a Chinese. I was Burmese by birth, but I was rarely allowed to forget that I was ethnically Chinese. This is one of the many paradoxical aspects of the native-foreigner relationship: the natives often mock and insult foreigners who choose to reside in their country permanently, but they invariably smile and welcome tourists who are there for a week or two.

The cemetery gate, which was made of rustic iron bars, could hardly keep anything in or out. But this was a place where those who came could never leave, and those who could leave wouldn't stay long, so any kind of gate—strong or weak—was purposeless. Several yards away from the gate was a pavilion. Found in every Chinese cemetery, this pavilion is to house the body temporarily before it is buried. Here, family members burn incense, say prayers, and bid the deceased farewell. They also burn paper rolls that serve as symbolic currency for the deceased. Provided bureaucracy in the underworld is efficient and free from corruption, the deceased will promptly receive the currency burnt in his or her name and he or she will be able to use it to purchase whatever is needed in the afterlife. It is, in a manner of speaking, wiring money from the mortal world to the underworld. But the Chinese don't stop at money; they also burn paper cars, paper houses, and even paper mansions complete with porches, gardens, and servants. Not even Western Union can deliver on such a grand scale.

After we had all gotten out of the car, a bony Burmese man approached us. His shirt, which might have once been bright red, was dingy brown. His sarong was worn high above his knees, exposing stiff, sinewy calves. He greeted my uncle, who recognized him immediately. He was the undertaker and the head of the family that lived and worked in this cemetery. Once a year, when my uncle came to pay homage to my grandfather, they would receive a portion of the food offerings, such as fruits and sweet-rice packages. And, before departing, my uncle would give them a few hundred kyats, which was generally known as *tea-money*. He, in return, would keep my grandfather's tomb clean and weed-free. He and his family survived all year round, for the most part, on tea-money and food offered to the dead by surviving relatives.

"You came early this year," he said; he knew it was not yet the Ghost Festival, the month Chinese families traditionally visit ancestral tombs.

"Yes," said my uncle, "I brought some relatives from America."

He hollered his family to come and help us carry our food plates and paper rolls. One by one, they all drifted out of the sea of dried grass where they had been squatting, carrying axes, picks, shovels and other tools of the trade. There were about a dozen of them altogether. The oldest one, probably the man's wife, was in her early forties. The youngest one, who I later learned was the man's granddaughter, was about seven or eight, wearing a canvas hat one size too big for her tiny head. The others, I gathered from conversations overheard, were the man's sons and daughters and their spouses. Like the surface of polished pebbles, their exposed skin glowed with a kind of bluish shine in the sun. They were dressed humbly. They were not in discolored rags, but there was something about their attitude that made them look faded, subdued. It was probably the humility with which they conducted themselves, knowing the red dust on their hands and feet could never be washed away.

"Where is Tai-pa-kong?" asked my uncle.

Tai-pa-kong is the mythical gatekeeper of cemeteries. It is believed that if sufficient offering is not made to him, he may hinder or interrupt a funeral procession. In the worst scenario, he may not let the funeral proceed at all. Therefore, upon entering a cemetery, the Chinese always appease him with some token offerings, even if they are not there to bury anyone. It makes sense to bribe him in advance—everyone has to come to him for permission sooner or later. Apparently Chinese bureaucracy works much the same way in the underworld.

"Tai-pa-kong is there," said the man, leading us to a little altar in front of the pavilion. We all followed him to the altar. My uncle placed a few oranges, bananas, and a bowl of rice on the altar. "Have you got your paper rolls?" asked the man. My uncle produced the paper rolls. "Then go ahead and *fong-pao*," he said. That took me by surprise. The term he had just used was a Chinese term, which described the act of making burnt offerings. Burmese are extremely nationalistic. Normally, a Burmese, whose attitude towards Chinese and Pakistanis is only slightly better than an old fashioned European's contempt and distrust for Jews, will neither learn nor speak the foreigners' languages. But here was a Burmese man, not only guiding us in our rituals like an expert, but also speaking in our despised language. This indicated to me that the man had been working here for a long time. That was the only reason he had managed to learn—perhaps against his will—the fine points of Chinese burial rituals and relevant Chinese phrases. I couldn't imagine the degradation this Burmese man felt working in a Chinese cemetery.

Having obtained permission from Tai-pa-kong, we proceeded to my grandfather's tomb. But we were detained for a while on our way; the wife came and told us that she had just noticed some bees in the vicinity of the tomb. Then she dispatched some of her family members—a team of six—to clear the area. The remaining team of six, each wielding a menacing weapon of some sort, surrounded us as we stood and waited. My father and I were carrying crisp $20 bills, whose total value in local currency probably exceeded anything this family had ever seen. There was no one nearby to observe what was happening. There were six of them and three of us; we were outnumbered two to one. My uncle held a match, and my father was balancing a small peeling knife in his hand. I had nothing to defend myself with beside my pen. I had heard that the pen was mightier than the sword, but could it be adequate defense against shovels, axes, and pitchforks? It was an uneasy situation. To make matter worse, one of the young men decided to make his comedic debut then; with a grin that revealed teeth stained with blood-red betel-juice, he delivered his brilliant one-liner: "Hey," he asked his audience, "doesn't it look like we are kidnapping a bunch of foreigners?" Nobody laughed; everyone glared at him.

With the bees driven away, we were told it was safe to proceed. So we did. There were more paper rolls burnt and more food offered. Mr. Chinchu had never been frugal; he was a generous soul, who liked to give unprecedented bonuses to his employees. He could use every roll of money we burned. So we didn't stop burning until we saw a swirling tornado of ash rising up from the ground. As I stepped back to avoid being in the path of the storm, I noticed the girl with the canvas hat skillfully leaping from one tomb to another. Her red skirt with polka dots flew in the afternoon breeze with every jump. Looking at this tiny creature performing her own unique brand of gymnastics, I realized she was at home in the cemetery. This was an unsettling notion because I never thought anyone could feel *at home* in a cemetery. I had never willingly visited a cemetery; the overwhelming evidence of mortality was just too much to bear.

"Be careful," I heard a paternal warning from the young man who had been watching her movements. "You might fall into a tomb through some cracks." It was as if he was warning her to stay away from junk food, or to wipe her hands on a towel instead of her skirt. But junk food and personal hygiene, it seemed, were not relevant here; she was not very likely to be able to afford a box of candies before mealtime, nor was she likely to have a towel devoted solely for her hands. His main concern, then, was her safety. And even that was not such a great concern because he knew that she had championed the art of tomb jumping.

"Does she go to school?" I asked. It was a silly way to start the conversation; it was a weekday afternoon, and she was evidently not sitting in a classroom. But the young man smiled forgivingly, ignoring my incredulity, and answered that she was not enrolled in any school.

"She had been sick the last two weeks or so," he said, "but she's recovering now." By then, sensing that she was the subject of our conversation, the girl approached us. I raised my camera to zoom in on her. She posed for me, kneeling on a lavish tomb of blue marble. That was when I noticed the watery eyes underneath the huge hat. I signaled her to come closer so I could get a better look at them. They were red and swollen.

"What's wrong with her eyes?" I asked.

"We don't know," answered the young man.

When he saw the concerned look on my face, he added, "It'll go away—it usually does." He made me wonder whether constant exposure to death made it easier to accept (and perhaps dismiss) human frailty.

The tempest of ash had subsided. We had seen what we had come to see. It was time to leave. My uncle gave some of the oranges, bananas, and sweet-rice packages to the head of the family. My father was counting out 500 kyats for tea-money. I added

200 kyats more, hoping the extra income might allow the father to buy the girl some medicines. (Later I learned that 700 kyats was barely enough for a visit to a doctor.) When the money was given, the man shut his eyes, his palms joined together in an upward position, and bowed. The gesture is known as *shikoe*. The Burmese use it to pray, and to express gratitude. Cab drivers and bus drivers *shikoe* when they come upon Sule Pagoda at the center of downtown Rangoon. Traffic is bad particularly downtown, with bumpers tapping against one another. But regardless of the speed they are traveling, or the number of lives entrusted in their care, those drivers will shut their eyes, release the steering wheels, and *shikoe*. In this brief moment of communal prayer, the cars and buses are driven by nothing but faith and faith alone. To me, *that* is putting their lives in God's hand.

As we were leaving the tomb, there was a commotion at the gate. I turned and saw that a series of cars had pulled in. "The Chan family is here," announced one of the young women. "They usually bring lots of food," said another excitedly. "They'll need help with the trays." This meant some more tea-money and some more food. In some ways, living with the dead has its advantages; the dead don't complain when their tombs are dirty, and they don't have much of an appetite, so they don't mind sharing their food with the undertaker's family. But how long could a family live on food for the dead and tea-money? What kind of existence was this? The dead had to live here because this was a cemetery. Did these men and women have to? Why couldn't they just leave? Actually, I already knew the answers.

The young men and women had gone off to the gate. The girl with the canvas hat, holding her father's hand, skipped all the way back to the gate with me. Then they both stopped a yard away from the gate—this was as far as they could go. I looked at the girl again, and I searched in my backpack for something. I knew I didn't have anything of value for her, but I felt like giving her something—someone had to give her something. And all I came up with was a box of after-coffee mints from Starbucks. It was not going to do a single thing to her swollen red eyes, but it was something. So I gave it to her. The girl looked at the blue-and-yellow tin box and smiled. I also smiled, knowing the little box would keep her happy for a time. Sooner or later, the colors on the box would fade, just like the polka dots on her red skirt, and she would become old enough to understand the utter uselessness of the tin box. But until then, she would be happy. And she deserved to be happy, because all she had otherwise was a field full of dead people.

My grandfather Mr. Chinchu, who was easily pleased to begin with, rested peacefully in the new Chinese cemetery on the edge of Rangoon. But I rested somewhat uneasily, knowing all the rivers of Burma could not wash the dirt off of this family.

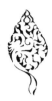

The Flower of the Orient

I have a weakness for pretty names. That was the reason I felt dizzy when I heard her name: Mala (Flower). For my brief and memorable encounter with this exquisite specimen of Burmese blossom, I owe much to the affable young men from Bagan Inn's housekeeping section.

Ever since they overheard me speaking Burmese on the phone, a few of the young men from the inn had been trying to experience vicariously through me the strip clubs of California and brothels of Nevada. A previous guest—an Australian backpacker by the name of Woody—had apparently predisposed this bunch of innocent Burmese to the ill-reputed (and thus more desirable) American establishments. I was told this modern day Casanova from down under chronicled his escapades with Polaroid shots of girls, some of them his victims, others willing participants of his exploits. My fluency in Burmese was a promise that I could succeed where Woody had failed—I could describe to them the intimate details of western mating rituals in their own native language. Woody provided the pictures; I would provide the text. So, while refilling the thermos or delivering my breakfast, the staff tried to bring up the subject. *So how much is it to get in? What do you do when you get in? What can you do? Are they pretty? Can you touch them? Can you invite them home? How much for an hour? How much for a night? How much for . . . How much to . . . What if I want to . . . .*

One evening, the young man who was returning my laundry asked, "Have you been to any of the clubs?" I assumed he was also after the same report. I bashfully told him, as I did to the rest of his dissatisfied colleagues, that I led a reclusive life among boxes of books in America and therefore knew very little of the establishments Woody frequented. He looked at me with dismay and said, "I was asking if you have been to the clubs in Rangoon." Now I looked at him in disbelief. Clubs in Rangoon? Impossible! When I was growing up, there was not a single nightclub in Rangoon.

"Are there any?" I asked dubiously.

"Oh yes," he assured me, "quite a few, and almost all of them feature fashion shows."

Fashion shows? Now I became curious. Recognizing the prospect of monetary compensation for his information, he proceeded to list the names and addresses of several clubs on a blank laundry bill. Two of them caught my attention because, judging from what I could still remember of Rangoon's general layout, they appeared to be located right in the middle of a produce market.

"Are you sure about these two? They seem to fall right in the middle of Thein Gyi Zei."

He gave me an affirmative nod.

"But how could that be? Thein Gyi Zei is an outdoor market."

"Not anymore," he replied with a meaningful wink.

Curious, I checked *Burma: Inside Guides*. There is no mention of nightclubs, but Thein Gyi Zei is described as a "wholesale fruit and vegetable market," where one could find "[m]ounds of red chillies and fragrant cinnamon bark, boxes of tropical fruits like mangosteen and durian, dried fish and seafoods *(sic)*, medicinal herbs and bottled concoctions, indigenous snacks treats to tempt the palate, and so much more."

It was late at night and I had nothing better to do. So I gave the young man a small tip and headed for the general vicinity of the market in a cab. Nothing could have prepared me for what I saw.

When my cab turned the corner, bright lights and neon signs nearly blinded me. All around me were bosomy girls with bold stares, smacking their painted lips. I was now in Rangoon's red light district, which I had never known to exist, within walking distance from the noodle stalls and incense booths of China Town. The tiny concentration of nightclubs flashed and danced with a frenzy no less intense than that with which its larger and bolder counterparts in Bangkok and Tokyo did. Heavy bass notes banged on the windows of my cab with an obnoxious beat. Swirling colors and patterns of light made me dizzy. Before I could tell my cab driver to turn around, a young man in a white shirt wearing a clip-on bow tie elbowed his way out of the crowd and pried open the passenger door beside me. Ignoring my protest, he dragged me out of the cab.

"Welcome to our club," he said, in English, Chinese, and what sounded like Japanese. To make sure his well-practiced tri-lingual greeting was not lost in the cacophony, he screamed directly into my ear. I told him he could speak to me in Burmese.

"I thought you were Japanese," he said, crestfallen.

"American," I clarified. "But I was born in Rangoon," I added hastily.

"That's actually better," he said, suddenly cheery and excited again.

He ushered me up the red-carpeted steps underneath a large neon sign. Lined up on both sides of the entrance, like friendly stewardesses beside a boarding gate, were two scores of tightly outfitted local girls. The young man, whose clip-on bow tie had become undone from all the pushing and shoving, snapped his fingers commandingly and I suddenly found myself flanked by two girls.

We boarded an elevator, operated by a gnomish Burmese man wearing a turban that covered half his face (and both his eyes). No one said a word to him, but he seemed to know instinctively which floor we wanted to get off on; with great weariness he chose and pressed a button. After a suspenseful period of noisy turbulence without any discernible vertical movement—a period the elevator operator cavalierly referred to as "warming up"—the ancient machinery took off, swinging side to side as it climbed upward. Even though I saw the button he had pressed, I couldn't tell which floor we were going to; the original characters on many of the buttons had long been effaced and some of the buttons were no more than twisted wires sticking out of empty sockets. During this rickety ride, the young man approached the two girls.

"You better take good care of him," he whispered to them in Burmese.

"Why?" asked the talkative one with ponytails.

"He's Japanese and he's got a *huge* wallet," the young man answered.

Japanese? What was he talking about? I tried to correct him, but he stopped me, signaling me to play along with his eyes. I was now the unwitting participant of his favorite sport—a game of deliberate misinformation at the expense of the girls.

"How do you know about his wallet?" the shy and evidently skeptic girl inquired under her breath.

"Saw it when he was paying the cab driver," he convinced her.

My wallet *was* huge; I was carrying a folded laundry bill, and photocopies of certain pages of my passport, as I had been instructed to do by the State Department's Web site, as proof my American citizenship.

In America, I am generally referred to as Asian-American. But depending on the degree of precision with which one wishes to acknowledge my heritage, I can also be a Chinese-American, a Burmese-American, or even a Chinese-Burmese-American. Back in Burma, I am an American, but one who is often mistaken for a Singaporean or a Malaysian, because I do not fit the profile of blond-haired, blue-eyed Americans in *Dynasty* and *Charlie's Angels*, two of the shows largely responsible for many Asians' notion of the champagne-sipping, Rolls-Royce-riding, partner-swapping Americans. This multi-cultural, multi-national identity of mine often makes me reassess my "ethnic origin" or my "nationality" whenever I fill out forms. I have no simple answer to the question "Who are you?" The answer sometimes depends on the form I am completing at the time. So, when I was offered a chance to adopt an entirely new identity, I immediately snatched it—Japanese was as good an identity as Indonesian or Cambodian. In a way, a new identity simplified things for me.

I bent down and bowed several times, imitating an affluent businessman from Tokyo or Osaka. The girls bowed back, both giggling. The gnome observed our interactions, glowering silently behind his turban. A few minutes later, I heard the girls whispering to each other in Burmese. *Japanese are rich—I'm sticking around. But you're supposed to be at the gate. Forget the gate—I don't make any money standing there flashing my teeth. I'm following him to his hotel—I haven't made enough for the night.* Suddenly it became clear to me. This was no fruit and vegetable market; this was a meat market.

"Want girls?" asked the bartender as he gave me my drink. I told him I was content with just my drink for the time being. I heard dance music but I saw no one on the floor, so I asked the bartender why no one was dancing. "The fashion show is about to begin," he said. And it began soon. The focus of the show, as it turned out, was not so much what the models were wearing but what they were *not* wearing. Each with a numbered badge, the girls walked down the central aisle, flaunting their slim, smooth limbs, wearing tight outfits in varying degrees of revelation. There were no Ungaro or Givenchy winter collections—only short skirts and elastic pullovers, designed to give the spectators a fairly good idea of how the models would look naked. But the girls knew how to walk the catwalk, swivel, and toss their hair seductively; a few of them even pouted like Claudia Schiffer. Then I noticed one girl standing at the far corner of the runway, biting her bottom lip. Something set her apart from the others. The other girls cast inviting glances at dressed-up patrons as they walked down the aisle, but she went through her routine passively.

"I don't know who she is," answered my bartender when I inquired. "She's very new." So I bribed him to make him more resourceful. After conferring with numerous other bartenders, he returned with her name. "Her name is Mala," he said. I felt like fainting. "Try the other ones," he advised; "she's not that friendly." At that moment, I heard clapping and cheering from the patrons gathered at the center. The volume of the music was turned up, and the floor suddenly became populated with guests leaping and bouncing in spotlights.

"The show is over," said the bartender. "The models will come out and dance now." So I waited. Before long, she reappeared in the dancing crowd, smiling and laughing. She was dancing with another girl. I wanted to cut in, but I didn't know what the protocol was in Rangoon. Then, I heard music from the speakers. Trine Bix, the lead singer from Daze, was singing in her coquettish nasal voice:

Voom va pa aya aya voom va pa o!
Voom va pa aya aya voom va pa o!
I need a superhero lover.
I need a superhero lover ayi yayi o!

I fancied my friend Aung Moe saying, "This is a sign!" For him, many ordinary things were signs—one only had to know how to interpret them. I interpreted mine favorably—that was the only way I could convince myself to cut in. So, braving 60 or 70 pairs of eyes, I walked across the dance floor and indicated to her with hand gestures that I wanted to dance with her. She nodded. The other girl didn't move away. Instead she moved aside, and continued dancing. I had no choice but to dance with both. And I did.

When we finally sat down together, she introduced the other girl to me. "This is my sister Moe Moe," she said. And Moe Moe, sensing that I wanted to be alone with Mala, excused herself and walked away. It was 45 minutes before closing time. I asked her if I could meet her afterwards. "It's too late," she said. But I insisted. "Call me tomorrow," she said, and scribbled her phone number and address on the laundry bill I had brought along. Suddenly, the music stopped and the lights came on. "The club is closed," she said. "Come, I'll walk you out." At the door, she leaned against the frame with a smile and watched me got into a cab.

Overzealous, I called as soon as I finished my breakfast. She answered in a sleepy voice. Realizing it was 7:30 in the morning, I apologized profusely for waking her up. "That's all right," she said. We agreed to meet in the evening in front of the club where we met the night before. A dozen red roses is not the customary gift to bring a girl on a date in Burma; the Burmese believe flowers are more suitable for shrines and pagodas. But I wanted to bring her something. I asked what her favorite snack was. "Apples," she said, "big red ones from the Chin Hills—I don't know why, but they always make me happy."

The Chin tribe, an ethnic minority, lives in the hilly regions in the northwestern part of Burma. Certain tribal rebels were reportedly still battling against the government troops in this region for autonomy. It would indeed be a heroic deed to fly to this region, where there was little assurance of safety for foreigners, to bring her back a dozen red apples. There might be an easier way to impress her. I asked what she liked to do in her free times. "I like to read Poe Zar," she confessed, giggling. "My mom is always telling me I spend too much time reading these silly books, but I like them—they're really funny. Do you read them? Have you read that one where . . .?" I was familiar with Poe Zar. He was a cartoonist whose books featured two mischievous sisters and their blundering bachelor uncle. I assumed his books could easily be found among the stalls of sidewalk booksellers on Shwe Bontha Road. I decided to go shopping for books that afternoon.

As it turned out, apples from the Chin Hills were sold by the crate in an open market within walking distance from the inn, so I went and bought a dozen. But the search for Poe Zar's books unexpectedly turned out to be as arduous a task as the quest for the Holy Grail. When I asked for his latest book, the first bookseller, who was squatting on the pavement with a steel mug overflowing with Indian milk-tea, produced something published three years ago, with unsightly brown stains on the cover that looked like curry sauce or betel juice, or a mixture of both. When I asked for something more recent in better condition, the second bookseller, who was sharing the first one's milk-tea, handed me a copy of the same book with a clean cover. I walked up and down Shwe Bontha Road, stopping before every stall large and small. It was lunch time, so every bookseller greeted me with a grin that revealed yellowish teeth partially covered with masticated meat and rice. But whenever I mentioned the name Poe Zar, the bookseller wiped off his grin (sometimes also the sauce on his chin) and shook his head. After prancing about for an hour or so between heaps of books, my Galahadean effort was rewarded with a thin bimonthly magazine containing several comic strips by Poe Zar—not exactly the Grail itself, but a piece of the Grail nonetheless, and certainly better than no Grail at all.

When I went to pick her up, I had a dozen shiny apples and a magazine with her favorite cartoonist's comic strips. I did feel a little bit like a gallant hero. She smiled gleefully when she noticed the gifts on the back seat of the cab. She was in her early twenties, but her dimples made her look even younger. I asked her how much time she could spare.

"Please bring me back here by ten-thirty," she said. "I have to be back here in time for the fashion show." That gave me only two hours—just enough time for us to have a meal and head back—nothing more. I suggested dinner, hoping I could, during the course of the meal, persuade her to meet me again afterwards. "Can I bring my sister along?" she asked.

Her insistence on the presence of a chaperon, I assumed, was her way of indicating that the evening was going to be a chaste one. That was somewhat different from what I had originally imagined, but I decided to continue with it; the headstrong knight in me wanted to cling to any possibility of romance even when it was apparent there wouldn't be any.

"My sister is babysitting the son of a friend at home," she said, and gave the cab driver instructions to get to their apartment. It is uncommon for two young girls to live on their own in Burma, so I asked her where her parents were. "My father passed away a year or so ago," she said, "and my mother has a place of her own near downtown."

When we arrived, she pointed out the flat where they lived, and hurried up the stairs, promising to return shortly. The cab was parked close to the sidewalk, so I could overhear her neighbors' conversation. *What's that foreigner doing here? Don't know, but he came with Mala. Probably someone she met at the club. Well, you know how those clubs are. They're all the same.* A bad reputation is like an ugly tattoo in Burma: everyone frowns on it, and it is nearly impossible to hide. I didn't know why, but I was genuinely concerned. I didn't want her to be branded as a *slut*. I felt protective towards her. So I rolled up the darkened windows, partly to remain invisible, and partly to block out the voices of the neighbors. It didn't help—I could still see their twisted lips, and I could read what they were saying. Twenty minutes later, I heard a tap on the window. I rolled it down, expecting to see Mala, but I saw Moe Moe instead, standing there and looking embarrassed. I asked her where Mala was.

"We need to ask you a favor," she said, "and Mala felt too awkward to ask you, so she sent me down instead." I asked her if everything was all right. "It's that boy," she explained. "He won't stop crying. I think we need to bring him back to his mom. So if it's all right, can we just . . . ." She asked, after an uneasy pause, if we could all just head back to the club, where the boy's mother was working. And the dinner plan? "We're not really hungry," she replied. But I was, so I had to devise a plan that would accommodate everything on our agenda—in the remaining one and a half hour.

"Let's bring the baby along with us to the restaurant," I suggested, "and after a quick meal, we'll all go back to the club." Moe Moe began to say something, but the cab driver—either because he felt bad about the way my date was turning out or because he saw a chance to extend the ride—interrupted her.

"I know a cozy little Chinese restaurant just around the corner," he said. Moe Moe scratched her head a few times, doubting the practicality of my plan. But time was running out, so I had to exercise my veto power. I asked her to go get Mala and the baby so that we could be on our way. She shrugged and hurried up the stairs. Five minutes later, Mala and Moe Moe returned, carrying a cheerful, cheeky boy, a diaper box, and a bottle of milk. They both offered profuse apologies but I had to cut them short to save time.

"This is Po Chit," introduced Mala, when we were heading for the restaurant. Po Chit didn't look like a baby who had been crying. He looked perfectly content. As she played with Po Chit, Mala prepared to put the bottle into his mouth.

"Don't give him the bottle," Moe Moe leaned over and whisper in Mala's ear. "He's been peeing nonstop." Mala put the bottle away, and asked how many more diapers were left. "One," was the alarming answer from Moe Moe. So *that* was the reason the baby had to be returned to the mother urgently. Two teenage sisters, a hungry bachelor, and a baby who was about to wet himself—we were beginning to look a lot like characters in a comic strip by Poe Zar. The cab driver, who had been silently listening to everything, was trying to suppress his smile. I saw the humor of the situation too, but I was not laughing; I began wondering how wise it was to bring this baby into the restaurant when the diaper supply was so dreadfully low. But I didn't have to wonder too long.

"Here we are," said the driver, pulling into the restaurant's parking lot.

Po Chit had a great sense of timing. He remained a perfectly lovely creature while we placed our order. But he began to fidget as soon as our dishes arrived. The two sisters debated whether he should be given access to the bottle. I tried to distract him by making faces, but unintentionally succeeded in scaring him into frantic squeals instead.

"Why don't I watch the baby while you eat?" offered the helpful waiter. To be fair, we warned him about the strong possibility of Po Chit's bodily discharges, but he was willing to take the risk; his luck turned out to be quite bad. Volunteering to babysit was only the first of his many mistakes during the evening. We had just sipped our first spoonful of soup when he returned with the baby in his arms and a wet spot on his vest. "Have you got any extra diapers?" he asked sheepishly. While Moe Moe was getting the diaper box, Po Chit reached over and pulled Mala's hair. Mala screamed. The waiter stepped back, but Po Chit wouldn't release his grip. Mala screamed again.

"Oh Lord!" cried the waiter. "Looks like he wants his mother."

"But I'm not the mother," cried Mala, which produced a horrified look on the waiter.

To misattribute parenthood to an unmarried girl may be no more than a blunder in America, but in Burma, where society has its own underhanded way of punishing impropriety, such a mistake is taken as a serious offense. The blushing waiter offered his apologies to Mala and then turned to Moe Moe, who was putting the diaper on Po Chit, and said, "Now you must be the mother."

"No I'm not," replied Moe Moe, doubling the poor waiter's embarrassment. More apologies followed. Then he turned to me—his only remaining choice and thus, he reasoned, a foolproof one. I realized I was about to become the proud father of Po Chit unless someone intervened. "He's not the father," cried the two sisters simultaneously before he could open his mouth again.

After we had returned Po Chit to his rightful mother, I had some time alone with Mala. "Maybe I'm imagining this," I said, "but I get the feeling you don't like working here."

"The girls are petty and competitive," she said. "They're always comparing the amount of tips they make or the number or wreaths they get." She showed me the wreaths, which were made of glossy papers. They came in gold and silver, one as gaudy as the other. "For 500 kyats," she said, "you can buy one of these wreaths and personally present it to your favorite model during the fashion show— that's how the club makes money." She wore one around her neck and, sticking her tongue out and rolling her eyes, pretended to get strangled. For 500 kyats, I thought, I could get her a dozen red roses from the market. I hated the thought that she had to parade around wearing artificial wreaths. I wanted to give her something *real*.

"I'm only going to be here for a month or two," she said, "and then I'll quit." She told me in confidence her modest ambition: "When I've saved up enough, I'll open a little cosmetic shop in the neighborhood—that way, I can go back to school."

"The last time I was here," I ventured, "the bartender said I could get girls. Do you know what he meant?"

"You can get girls here," she replied indifferently. "Do you want me to find one for you?" I decided it was best to remain silent.

I was finally beginning to understand her. She had to know that the club engaged in some unsavory trades ("Number fourteen, our sultry model Mala, in a fitted black blouse with low neckline . . ." "Want girls?"). This was a place where bartenders offered girls to their patrons more often then they did peanuts, and models followed patrons to their rooms and remained there till dawn for a certain fee. Working there, she learned to give in just enough to receive sufficient tips. She also acquired the skill to tactfully back away at the last possible moment without offending a patron. Hers was an act of balancing— as delicate as that of a tightrope walker. If she fell, she would fall right into the arms of salivating wolves below. And apples from Chin Hills and books by Poe Zar were, in a way, her psychological safety net—so long as she could cling to them, she could preserve her innocence, her childhood. But she knew she would have to grow up and give in to the adult world sooner or later.

"I've got to go," she said when the lights began to dim and flash. "The fashion show is going to start soon." I understood that our date had come to an end. I rang her up again the next morning, and asked if I could see her. "Can you come pick me up around three at our apartment?" she asked. I told her I could, but I was concerned with how it might appear to her neighbors. "Don't come out of the cab," she suggested. "I'll wait for you at the bottom of the stairs."

The same afternoon, I walked to the market several blocks away from my inn in search of fresh flowers. Between large tables filled with bloodied kidneys and writhing catfishes, I found a stall full of fragrant roses—pink, white, yellow and velvet-red. I asked the woman behind the booth to pick a dozen red ones for me and leave their long stems uncut.

"But you won't be able to fit them into the shrine," she cautioned. I told her they were for a girl—not for a shrine. Encouraged by the personal information I had just volunteered, she proceeded to ask if they were for a *bo ma lay* (a white girl). I told her they were for a Burmese girl. "We don't do this kind of thing here," she said, trying to dissuade me from making an all-too-American gesture to a wholesome Burmese girl, as she wrapped the roses in a huge banana leaf. But I had my own reason. From the beginning, I had wanted more than a companion for a few nights: if that was all I had wanted, I would have enlisted the help of the bartender who asked, "Want girls?" I wanted a fairy tale. I was looking for a chance to be the knight from a faraway kingdom who came to the rescue of a provincial damsel in distress. So an all-too-American gesture was just fine.

When I arrived, there was no one waiting at the bottom of the stairs. I remembered the window she had pointed out to me as hers the previous day. Promising a generous tip, I persuaded the cab driver to go up and ask for her while I waited. A moment later, I heard a tap on the window. I rolled down the window and there was Moe Moe again. She leaned in, looking apologetic.

"Our mother has just arrived unannounced," she said. "Mala wouldn't be able to come down." I asked if I should come back later. "The thing is," she said, "we really don't know how long our mother is staying." I felt lost. "But call Mala again later," she suggested. I promised her I would. But I never did; I came to the conclusion that two teenage sisters and a bachelor old enough to be their uncle should not be anything else other than characters in an amusing anecdote.

Flowers are real: they have physical and tangible properties. Therefore, like everything else physical and tangible, they are bound to wither and die. But one can also offer them to a shrine, and remember them forever for their grace and purity. This way, they remain forever fresh in one's memory. And this, I believe, is the Burmese way.

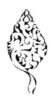

The Flight of the Peacock

When I told the receptionist at the inn that I wanted to visit Inle Lake in Shan State, he gave me the names and addresses of a few tour-bus operators and a train schedule.

"What about planes?" I asked. He immediately shrank.

"Domestic carriers are unreliable," he replied.

So there were occasional delays. That was nothing new to me. But apparently, there was more. "They frequently crash," he added, grimacing to suggest the dreadful frequency with which these crashes occurred. But if I was determined to fly, he continued reluctantly, I could fly on one of the two domestic airlines—Yangon Airways and Air Mandalay—to Heho Airport, from where I could proceed to Inle Lake by car or coach. "But they're the same," he warned, meaning one airline's safety record was no more impressive than that of the other. But I was desperate. I wanted to leave Rangoon as quickly as possible. For nearly a week I had waited patiently for its climate to change for the better, but it only got worse—it got hotter. I had to shower and change

three times a day, and my pants and shirts stayed in
the inn's laundry room longer than they did on me.
It was time to escape to the cold highlands of Shan
State. I had heard so many songs and stories cele-
brating the beauty of fair-skinned Shan maidens
that I felt like meeting one myself. Perhaps I might
be inspired to compose a poem of my own: "Ode to
a Shan Beauty."

"Which one of the two airlines," I asked the receptionist, "is the better one?" He remained in silent
deliberation for a considerable length of time. Finally,
just as my adventurous self was about to yield to
my judicious self, he announced the winner: Yangon
Airways. Curious, I looked around for the reason he
had picked Yangon over Mandalay. And I found what
might have been his reason, in the *Business Yellow
Pages of Rangoon*. The slogan of Yangon Airways was,
"You're safe with us." Air Mandalay gave no such
guarantee. Its slogan was simply, "The Golden Flight."

"It's true," confirmed my friend Nay Moe, who
worked for an air-ticketing agent's office on
Pansoeden Street in downtown. "They periodically
crash." But if I really wanted to go, he continued, not
only could he make all the necessary arrangements
for me, but he could also book my ticket and room
at the rate for local residents (which was nearly half
off the rate for foreigners). "And don't worry," he
reassured me. "You'll be fine." *The Karen rebels bomb
trains whenever they want to make a political statement,
but if you need to take the train, take the train—you'll be
fine. There is a fire in the next district but it'll have to burn
several blocks lined with brick buildings before it gets to
us, so it may not even get to us at all—we'll be fine.* The
Burmese believe that those with good karma will

survive regardless, and those with bad karma won't. And everyone believes—or wants to believe—that his or her karma is better than that of the person in the next seat or the person who lives next door. This is not fatalism. This is typical Burmese optimism. And apparently it was infectious—I decided to gamble against my better judgment.

"Go ahead and plan a weekend trip for me," I told my friend Nay Moe.

The next day, he came to me with the itineraries and gave me a summary of the entire trip. I would fly to Heho Airport, where a guide carrying a sign would meet me. The name on the sign should be mine, but there was a possibility it might just read Nay Moe. In either case, he was my guide and he would take me to my hotel, where I might once again find myself registered under the name Nay Moe. His attempt to book the ticket and the room at the discounted rate, explained my friend, had resulted in some minor clerical confusion. I told him I didn't mind; I liked the idea of traveling incognito. That was what the Burmese kings did (according to folk tales, at any rate) when they had had enough with the lies and flatteries of their courtiers and ministers, and decided they would see for themselves how the commoners were living.

On the same evening, the plan continued, I would visit Pindaya, where I would see countless images of Buddha carved on the walls of a cave. The following morning, I would navigate through the famous floating market of Inle Lake, where transactions were conducted mostly on the prows of sampans and boats. I would also be visiting, as a short excursion, the renowned monasteries in the region, including "Jumping Cat Monastery," where I would have a chance to see (of course) a cat that could jump. A cat that could not jump, in my view, would have been really worth seeing. "No, no," clarified my friend, "this cat can jump through flaming hoops." Then, my question was, why was this talented creature not in a circus? But kitty show or no kitty show, the mere thought of being in a milder climate got me excited. Then I was handed my ticket, which came in an elegant red envelope with the picture of a magnificent creature with out-stretched feathers. The white lettering, shadowed in gold, read, "Air Mandalay: The Golden Flight." "You're going to be fine," reassured my friend, as he left hurriedly.

When I informed my other friends that I would be flying out to Shan State, they reacted much in the same way the inn's receptionist did—they cringed. They did not raise any objections but, with great subtlety, they posed a series of questions to hint their concern. *Fly? Why fly? Wouldn't you rather go by train or bus? For the same amount of money, you can rent a van and drive up to a nearby beach resort. Ever been to Chaungtha? No? It's a lovely beach. You'd love it there. Why, we can even accompany you the entire trip if you go to Chaungtha.* Then they lamented the loss of their former neighbor—a Pakistani stewardess who died in a recent plane crash. *So young. So pretty. Sad, isn't it? What did they say happened? Turbulence? The poor husband is still grief-stricken.* But, assuming my karma was better than that of the unfortunate stewardess, they all made a unanimous proclamation in the end—I would be fine.

Mingaladon Airport, the country's only international airport, was recently blessed with a new extension—a terminal with a spire. With climbing curves and dangling spikes, it stood next to the aviation tower, one as much in harmony architecturally with the other as Dalai Lama was with Chairman Mao politically. I suspected that the new terminal was supposed to give the airport a certain palatial look. The resulting look, however, was more monastic than majestic. *Mingaladon: the Monastery of the Flying Airplanes.*

"Ticket please," demanded a scrawny army officer at the entrance, as if he were admitting me to a movie. Having examined my plane ticket, he allowed me to proceed. "Where're your tickets?" he asked my father and my cousin, who had come to see me off. "Sorry," said the officer, "only those with tickets can enter." He shut the door behind me. So that was it—no ticket, no show. I told my father and my cousin I would call them from Heho Airport, and went in alone. But we learned later that he—or anyone on duty at the gate—would have smuggled us in at the rate of 200 kyats per person.

The physical space of the airport itself was so small that there was hardly any room for error. There were two entrances: left and right. There were two terminals: Foreign and Domestic. The left entrance led to the Foreign Terminal, and the right to Domestic. As I watched, this dual option was reduced to a single option—after being informed that there were no more foreign planes scheduled to land for the day, a guard festooned a steel chain and shut the Foreign Terminal down with a cardboard sign that read "closed." But this drastic minimalism, which was meant to simplify operations, seemed to backfire sometimes, causing confusion and disorder.

"Ticket please," asked the officer at the gate when a blond English girl with delicate features approached him. She didn't understand what ticket he was demanding so she tried to walk past him. He blocked her path and repeated, "Ticket please." She slapped the small zipper bag around her waist to indicate that her ticket was inside. By then, a few onlookers were beginning to form a circle, and another officer had joined the commotion. An exchange began in Burmese between the officers.

"What's going on?"

"I think she's trying to tell me her ticket is inside."

"Just let her come in then."

"I can't. I have to see her ticket."

"What for?"

"I need to direct her to the right terminal."

"Well, she's obviously a foreigner, so . . . ."

They directed her to the Foreign Terminal, which was, of course, closed. A few minutes later, the girl returned, flushed in anger, gesticulating the way I had never seen an English girl do.

"For God's sake," she cried, "I'm late for my flight now."

"What happened?" asked the officer.

"That terminal is closed," she said, pointing behind at the sign with her thumb. The other officer returned. Once again a discussion began in Burmese between the two.

"Who closed that terminal?"

"Don't know. No one told me it's closed."

"Do you know where she's going?"

"No, I didn't get to see her ticket."

"Let's ask her again. She may be flying domestic."

"Ticket please," said both officers in English.

With outstretched arms, a young porter in a frayed blue-uniform shuffled towards me in sandals. "Sir," he said, gently pulling my bag, "let me carry your bag." My duffel bag, which contained nothing but three sets of clothing and my toiletries, was light enough to be tossed around by a bunch of school-boys. I was about to tell the young porter I didn't need his service when I realized that he was about the age of a schoolboy. Perhaps I should let him earn a few hundreds kyats so he could return to his classroom rather than work as a carrier, I thought. So I released my grip, whereupon he began to drag my bag alongside. When we found an empty spot on a wooden bench, he attempted to make small talk.

"You Japanese? Chinese?" he asked, trying to guess. This would be an uncomplicated exchange for most tourists. A Japanese tourist would confirm that he was Japanese and tell this youth about nightclubs in Tokyo. A Chinese tourist would confirm that he was Chinese and proudly describe the Forbidden City or the Great Wall to the curious youth. But what was simple for them was not so simple for me. I would have to explain to this youth that I was ethnically Chinese, but I knew nothing of China because I had been living in America. I could, of course, tell him something about Burma, my birthplace, but it would hardly be of any interest to him. For a second or two, I seriously thought of using by borrowed identity: *Hi, my name is Nay Moe, and I live in Rangoon.* It would have made things much simpler.

Beyond the custom checkpoint, there was a waiting room with segregated seating. One section of the room was marked "Nationals" with a sign mounted on a pole. The other section was marked "Foreigners," with a similar sign of a slightly larger scale. I looked around and immediately noticed that those who were sitting in the Nationals section were mostly sandy-haired Westerners, and those in the Foreigners section mostly sarong-clad Burmese men and women. In a way, it was understandable. Most tourists are curious to find out how the natives really live, and most natives want to live the hotel-dwelling, nightclub-hopping life of a wealthy New York stockbroker on vacation. So, when given a choice, tourists choose to become natives and natives choose to become foreigners, at least for as long as they feel comfortable in their adopted roles. But I wasn't sure to which of the two sections I belonged more. My plane ticket was purchased at the discounted rate for a Burmese national, but I held an American passport. I was—in a manner of speaking—having an identity crisis. So I did what I thought best: I stood over the line that divided the two sections, with one foot in each.

I overheard intimate whispers in mellifluous French from a man and a woman standing nearby. The couple was accompanied by a young lady of extraordinary elegance, wearing a gilded, hand-woven sarong and a fitted, long-sleeve blouse. No one would endure the discomfort of such an elaborate outfit unless she was a bride, a calendar model, or a professional tour-guide. The absence of a groom (a gentleman in an equally regal outfit and a turban) or an entourage of fans and photographers, indicated to me that she was a tour-guide.

There was also a man—with the characteristic milky smooth skin of a Shan—in a wheelchair, tended by another who appeared to be his personal physician. Being sufficiently sedated for the flight, the patient sat semi-conscious in his chair. But his physician, on the other hand, desperately needed sedation. After perfunctorily checking the patient's pulse and heart rate, he began pacing back and forth, and smoking one cigarette after another. Watching him trying to locate his lighter, which he forgot he had hidden in a small pouch inside his attaché case, was like watching a Charlie Chaplin skit with sound effects—with the jerky motion of an actor in a silent feature, he padded himself from chest to knee, and then from knee to chest, while cursing under his breath.

Suddenly, I heard a loud roar in the sky. The glass plates, which were held in a number of places by brown tape, began to shake and rattle as if they were about to shatter. The Shan's physician, instead of stepping back, stepped forward to catch a glimpse of the logo on the tail of the descending plane. But the sun was in his eyes so he couldn't see. He cursed. When the plane had landed on the runway, I saw what appeared to be a winged elephant on its tail. Why not? If a jumping cat could get a monastery of its own, a flying elephant certainly deserved an airline of its own. "Yangon Airways," hissed the doctor, following it up with some verbal monstrosities. Then I heard another roar and saw a second plane slowly descending from the cloudless sky. On its tail, I saw the same gold-and-red logo that appeared on my plane ticket. On its wings however, I saw something that I was accustomed to seeing only in black-and-white war movies—a pair of propellers. After it had successfully landed, it slid back and forth on the runway to stabilize itself. "Ah," cried the doctor happily, "Air Mandalay!" But this transformation from Hyde to Jekyll was short-lived; realizing he had run out of cigarette, he emerged once again from his own cloud of smoke an angry creature.

Buried in the wall behind us were several loud-speakers, their rustic green as old as uniforms worn by the English officers who had perished in some forgotten bunker while fighting the advancing Japanese army during World War II. In fact, those speakers looked like they had been rescued from an old bunker and then, instead of being given early retirement or honorary discharge, were forced back into active duty. Their screens were covered in a fine coat of dust that had not been disturbed since the Japanese surrendered. So I began to wonder whether they were still in a condition to answer if they were called upon.

I knew the moment had arrived when a uni-formed pilot from Yangon Airway came in with a clipboard that appeared to hold the passenger list. I watched him supervise the porters as they wheeled the luggage out into the airfield. He was a muscular Burmese with good stature. His dark skin and white uniform gave him an air of contradiction. When he saw that the luggage had been loaded onto the plane, he wiped the betel-juice trickling down from the corner of his mouth, and cleared his throat. Poised in a sunlit spot, he prepared to deliver his soliloquy. In a moment, I thought, I would hear his booming voice through those historic loudspeakers. The old boys would come back to life, once again, like the unbreakable soldiers from *The Bridge of the River Kwai*. But something didn't look quite right— the pilot had no microphone.

Those who are leaving for Sitwe on Yangon Airways flight number . . . .

The announcement came, not from the speakers, but straight from the mouth of the pilot—with his hands cupped around his mouth, he hailed, in a quivering staccato that was nothing like the voice of Sir Alec Guinness. Suddenly passengers began marching. With the merciless sun beating down upon them, they marched across the airfield in a queue, many of them weighed down by bags and baskets in their hands and on their shoulders. No one was whistling but a few of them, I noticed, were praying.

Anyone else going to Sitwe?

The pilot circled the room and continued to shout, with veins throbbing in his neck. All along, the loudspeakers, with their dignified silence, eloquently said, "We want no part of it."

It was 15 minutes before departure time. I felt like I needed some food to help me cope with this anticlimax I had just experienced. At the far end of the room, I saw a varnished wooden sign that read Airport Oriental House. I remembered a sumptuous feast—of countless plates of Chinese dumplings— that my father, my uncle, and I had enjoyed two days ago in the city. I distinctly recalled the name of the restaurant: it was Oriental House. The one inside the airport, undoubtedly, was a smaller branch of the one in the city. I approached the counter with high hopes. A bashful Burmese girl came forward to serve me.

"Can I get dim sum here?"

"Yes sir."

"What do you have?"

"We have steamed chicken, steamed pork, and a few others."

"Some egg rolls please?"

"Sorry, sold out. Try the steamed chicken."

"Thanks, but I think I'll take some steamed shrimps instead."

"Sorry, couldn't get shrimps at the market today. But steamed chicken is good."

The Burmese are too polite and too embarrassed to tell a visitor that he or she doesn't have any options. So they offer options that are not actually there to begin with, and gently guide the visitor back to the only option there is. *We don't subscribe to* The Guardian *or* Working People's Daily, *but try* The New Light of Myanmar—*you won't know the difference. Yangon Airways is better than Air Mandalay, but you'll be flying Air Mandalay. There are two terminals but one of them is closed for the day. We know you want egg rolls or shrimps, but try the chicken.* I ordered two plates of steamed chicken. The girl lifted out of the steaming pot eight dumplings, each smaller than a sun-dried prune. I finished my Lilliputian meal in two bites.

I noticed that the French couple was beginning to look uncharacteristically restless. The guide was trying to explain something to them, but they were shaking their heads and pointing at their watches. I looked at my watch, and saw that it was now 15 minutes past departure time. Outside, a Fokker plane with Air Mandalay's logo sat in the sun, like an actor in costume waiting for his cue. Our pilot was nowhere to be found. Our air-hostesses stood gathered in the corner, facing the wall and talking among themselves, clandestine and conspiratorial. The French couple's guide went over to them, and asked if they knew why we were not boarding the plane. They vehemently shook their heads. With matching outfits and buns, they looked like a bunch of wooden toys with springy heads—the kind tourists usually bring home as souvenirs. The guide went back to her clients and gave them the update, which was no update at all.

Jekyll, who wasn't around much to begin with, left Hyde fully in possession of the physician tending the Shan in the wheelchair. There were no more profanities because he had employed every conceivable one of them earlier. He was trying to get one of the porters to go out to the field and bring back his luggage. "There are expensive medicines," he screamed, "that shouldn't remain in the heat for too long." And the frightened porters went out to look for his bag in the heap of bags sitting in the sun. While they struggled to drag his bag out from the bottom of the pile, he paced in and out of a cloud of smoke, talking to himself. Nothing, it seemed, could induce Jekyll to return now.

It was 30 minutes past departure time, but there was still no news, no announcement, no explanation—nothing. But there were whispers among passengers. *What's going on? Well, something fell off inside the plane; one of the engineers is saying it needs to be fixed before the plane can take off again. Think they can fix it in time? In time for what? We're already late. Do they have a spare plane? No, I don't think so. They'll probably put us on the next flight. Yeah—we'll be fine.* And the whispers, it seemed, were almost as reliable as any official announcements, especially in the absence of one. When it was 45 minutes past departure time, which was when we were originally scheduled to land in Heho, the air-hostesses came to us and told us—as discreetly as possible—that our flight had been canceled.

We were herded back to Air Mandalay's counter. We were told we could obtain a refund for our tickets, or we could fly the following evening. I checked my itineraries. If I were to fly the following evening, my trip would exclude Pindaya Cave and Inle Lake, leaving me with only the kitty show at Jumping Cat Monastery. I told the lady behind the counter I wanted refund. "Where did you get the ticket?" she asked, without the slightest hint of an apology. I named my friend's office on Pansoeden Street. "Then," she said, "you'll have to go back there to get your refund." Before I had a chance to voice my dissatisfaction, she called the French couple behind me to come forward. Perhaps the Burmese happily pay to see a cat that can jump because it does precisely what it is supposed to do. In a place where loudspeakers are quiet and planes are grounded, a cat that can jump is a marvel.

I was irritated. And I was still not sure whether this had been a tragedy or a comedy. My father, like an experienced diamond cutter, knew how to dissect a situation and see it from the brightest possible angle: "I guess it was better," he said, "that the plane didn't take off at all. Being stranded in Rangoon is not as bad as being stranded in Shan State or being in a crash." He was right. Perhaps I ought to be just thankful that it ended in a comic note when it could have easily turned into a tragedy.

"What happened?" asked the young porter when I returned to the lobby in search of a phone. I told him I needed a ride back to my inn, because my flight had been canceled. "Are you coming back to catch the next flight?" he asked. I told him I wasn't. "So you Chinese?" he repeated his question, which went unanswered earlier. I took a deep breath. The moment of truth! The great revelation! I told him I came from America, but I was born in Burma. I waited for his reaction. He frowned, looking serious. Having processed the information, he rendered his judgment: "Then you're Burmese," he said. Curious, I asked him how he came to this conclusion. "Well," he replied, with the impatient tone of a math teacher who had just been asked why two plus two equaled four, "you were born here. That makes you Burmese." I asked him if he had factored in my legal status as an American citizen. I also told him that both my parents were Chinese. He shook his head, and put up his hand, as if to say, "I'm not interested." He was not about to let me complicate his simple equation. $E=MC^2$—*take it or leave it!* Identity, to this young genius, had everything to do with where one was born, and nothing to do with where one had been living or what one's parents' were.

When one of my former classmates came to visit me at the inn, soaked in sweat and covered in dirt, I offered him a cold beverage of his choice. I showed him the content of the refrigerator in my room, and asked him to pick what he wanted. Without looking, he said, "Just give me something in a bottle." The inn stored two kinds of bottled drinks: Star Cola, which tasted like Coca Cola, and Crusher, which tasted like Sunkist. "Either one is fine," he said. I gave him Diet Coke in a can instead. He drank it with indifference, and pronounced that it was fine.

When a Burmese child is born, a monk prepares a *zarta*—the course of the child's life as foretold by the position of the dominant planets at the hour of the child's birth. ("He grows up to become a murderer because he has the *zarta* of a murderer.") The first alphabet of a Burmese child's name is determined by the day of the week on which he or she is born. ("Nay Moe is your name? Born on a Saturday, weren't you?") A Burmese student does not often get to study what he or she is interested in; his or her scores from the matriculation exam narrow the choices down to two to three subjects. ("I have always wanted to be an engineer, but my scores aren't high enough; I am qualified to study Botany, History, or Philosophy.") A Burmese couple's wedding date is picked by a monk or an astrologer; the preference of the bride and the groom is often the least of the concerns. ("His hour of birth being that of the sacred serpent Naga, and hers being that of the mythical bird Garuda, he risks being devoured by her if they were to wed while Saturn is still within the shadow of the Sun.")

A Burmese is taught to believe that the misery he or she endures or the luxury he or she enjoys is the result of his or her karma. A Burmese is too alien to the concept of free will. Ask a Burmese to choose between karma and free will, and he or she will freely choose karma. The concept of karma offers a certain kind of peace; when one accepts that one's previous deeds predetermine one's future, one is no longer pressured by the constant need to guess and shape one's future.

In America, I have to make half a dozen or more decisions just to order a meal. ("We have beef, turkey, or tofu burger." "Cheese or no cheese?" "Swiss, Jack, or American?" "Want mustard, mayo, or lettuce on it?" "Pickle?" "Coca Cola or Pepsi?" "Diet or regular?" "For here or to go?" "Cash or charge?") At times, I wish my life were as simple as an equation or a chart. Burmese simplicity was a welcome change— once I had readjusted myself to it. I have become too American to relinquish the burden to choose. But I am still Burmese enough to relish an occasional freedom from choices. It was nice, for a change, to let someone else decide what I was. The young porter of Mingaladon had spoken: I was Burmese, he declared. And that was fine with me.

Francis of Assisi

I was riding—instead of a motorized sampan skipping across the lake at high speed in the cold highlands—a taxi inching along one of the busiest streets in downtown in the sweltering afternoon heat, stuck to a ripped vinyl seat with my own sweat. I was on my way to the ticketing agent's office on Pansoeden Street to collect a refund for the canceled flight. But I was now trapped in a traffic jam. On one side of the street stood the High Court building, a distinct Victorian structure in red and white bricks, complete with arches, domes, and a clock-tower that presided over downtown. On the opposite side of the street camped an army of pavement booksellers, some crouching with green cheroots disdainfully dangling from their mouths, others with heavy satchels swinging on their drooping shoulders.

"What's happening up there?" asked my cab driver to another one coming from the opposite direction.

"Someone—some high school student—fell from a bus and got ran over by a car," replied the other driver, shaking his head somberly.

Sadly, this was not uncommon. I used to ride the Number Nine bus to school—a line notorious for accidents. Usually, the bus was a lorry, floored with loosened wooden planks that shifted to reveal the street underneath at every turn. I had seen numerous rubber sandals fall through the gaps between planks. ("Aung Moe, what happened to one of your sandals?" "I think I dropped it through that hole.") The bus was always filled beyond its maximum capacity with passengers spilling out of both the front and back exits, clutching the handrails and hugging one another. During monsoon season, when the rails were wet and the steps slippery, the journey was literally a matter of life and death for those suspended riders.

When I noticed that pedestrians on the sidewalk were moving faster than the cars, I got out of the cab and joined them. I stopped before one bookseller and glanced at his collection of paperbacks, mostly Penguin or Bantam editions with yellowish pages, displayed on a mat only slightly larger than the top of a coffee table. Some familiar names, which belonged to different genres and eras and would normally be found separated by three or four shelves in a library, huddled together at my feet in the most intimate manner: *The Tommyknockers* by Stephen King, with horrifying weight, collapsing on a fragile copy of *The Old Man and the Sea*; Jane Austin's *Sense and Sensibility*, with neither pride nor prejudice, leaning on *The Bourne Identity* by Robert Ludlum; *The Tragedies of Shakespeare*, an oversized hard-bound edition, serving as the solid foothold on which Ian Fleming and Tom Clancy both rested.

Hiding in shame underneath a pile of robust James Bond books was a copy of Orwell's *Burmese Days*, its mutilated spine as hideous as the birthmark on the cheek of Orwell's hero Flory. It was brought into view by the bookseller's accidental kick that toppled the stack of Bond books and sent the unlucky Dr. No fighting for life on the edge of a nearby sewer. Finding *Burmese Days* in Burma as the result of a canceled flight and a series of accidents was, I thought, a bit uncanny. Two weeks after I bought it, I was to discover that the book was not merely deformed but also dismembered: pages between 136 and 153 were missing. A quarrel between the hero and the heroine at the bottom of 136 was immediately followed by an exclamation from an angry doctor at the top of 153 ("It was the first time they had definitely quarreled. He was too miserable even to ask himself how it was that he" immediately followed by "'Oh? What?' To Flory's surprise the doctor made such a violent gesture of anger . . ."). But standing over it at the time, I couldn't help but believe that I was destined to find this book. So I decided to rescue Orwell's moth-gnawed masterpiece, which might otherwise follow *Dr. No*'s fate and drown in the sewer the next time the bookseller took a wrong step.

Inspired by this unexpected discovery, I decided to get lost. My visit to the highlands of Shan State had been forfeited, indefinitely, so I had all the time I needed to get lost and find my way back. By getting lost, I had hoped to discover something new about the city. There were surely many secrets the city had not revealed to me yet. And they would never be revealed to me unless I was willing to abandon myself to it without reservation or preconception. Otherwise, I would only see what every other foreigner saw.

Returning from Pansoeden Street, I asked the cab driver to take an alternate route. I waited until I began to see landmarks that I didn't recall ever seeing before. When I was sure that I was in an unfamiliar neighborhood, I stopped the cab and got out to walk. I was in a residential neighborhood with single-story buildings for the most part. Relying on nothing but bad intuition, I wandered through short lanes, making random turns at every intersection. I passed a whitewashed mosque, near whose entrance hung numerous clotheslines sagging under the weight of checkered sarongs and soiled undershirts. And I passed a school, from whose shuttered windows I heard a chorus of boys and girls:

Nya a kha,
La tha tha,
Kasar malar nar malar.
A fine night,
The moon is bright,
Will you play or will you rest?

The teacher led the recitation, singing the nursery rhyme in the high-pitched tremolo of a nervous soloist. The students, like an ill-rehearsed choir performing a mass, repeated the rhyme in their screechy voices in various keys and tempos. Twenty-five years ago, mine was one of those screechy voices; the same rhyme was in the textbook I studied. I didn't remember ever seeing this school or the mosque, so I was fairly confident I was lost. That was when I found myself standing several yards away from a huge overhead sign that read, "Saint Francis of Assisi Catholic Church."

The church was a modest structure in red bricks, with a colonnade, a tower, and a huge circular stained-glass window at the center of its gabled façade. Sitting inside the wooden booth that looked like a sentry box, which was next to the gate, was a thin dark man with South Indian features. When I walked past him, I thought I would be stopped and questioned. But he just looked at me with a pair of baleful eyes from behind his glasses, which were as thick as the bottom of a wine bottle. I looked back, and was somewhat startled by a pair of disproportionately large eyes, swimming behind two black square frames like a couple of goldfishes in two separate tanks. We exchanged nods and I walked on.

I knew this humble church in the outskirts of an Asian city was far removed from the quiet stone cloisters in the Italian countryside where Francis of Assisi and his followers began their monastic order, and the climate of Southeast Asia a cruel punishment compared to that of Western Europe. A friar, of this or any other order, had no business walking around in a thick hooded habit in this heat unless he was doing penance for his mortal sins, committed during this and ten previous lives. So I wasn't expecting any robed friars when I walked through the gate. But I found one, standing with both arms outstretched in a gesture of indiscriminate embrace.

I walked towards the end of the main road where he stood. He was looking down from a raised platform, and he was made of marble. The compassion in his face, however, was made of the same stuff of which saints and martyrs are made. At his feet, there was an iron plate, with inscriptions identifying him as Francis of Assisi, founder of the Franciscan Order of Italy, in both Burmese and English. So the man was there, at least in stone if not in flesh and blood.

The doors of the main entrance were shut tight. I walked around the church, trying to find a side door that was open. I found two but they were barred and locked. I began looking around for an authority figure—someone in a cleric collar and a black outfit—to whom I could introduce myself. A couple of yards away from the church, I saw a group of men, whose features told me they were Burmese and Indian, sitting in the shade of a banyan tree. Two of them were playing checkers, moving small pieces of rocks on squares chalked up on a wooden stool. One of them, an Anglo-Indian man wearing a batik shirt of brown and red, was resting in a stretchable wooden hammock, playing with a Burmese boy about eleven. I heard occasional laughter from the two of them. There was something paternal about his behavior towards the boy. Having grown up in Rangoon, I could easily tell an urban youth from a provincial one. The boy was—both in attire and mannerism—unmistakably provincial. When our eyes met, both the man and the boy acknowledged me with smiles and nods.

I decided to return to the man inside the sentry box. After all, I reasoned, he was positioned to receive visitors as they arrived, so he ought to be the right man to turn to for information or permission of any kind. He watched me from behind his extraordinarily thick glasses as I approached. Once again, I found myself mesmerized by his gigantic eyes. The world, I thought, probably looked infinitely greater to him than it actually was. I greeted him in English. I got a nod, but there was no verbal response. I made another attempt, in Burmese. I got another nod, but there was still no verbal response.

"Please speak louder," he finally said, after a cough, when I was close enough to see my own reflections in his pupils. "I can't hear too well."

"How are you feeling?" I asked in Burmese.

"So so," he replied, rocking his head side to side. "Sometimes I feel fine, but sometimes I feel sick."

We often ask someone how he or she is feeling, but we seldom expect an honest answer. His, I realized, was an honest reply. There was no self-pity in his tone. It was one that suggested he had come to terms with whatever he was feeling—sick or well, he felt just fine. At this point, the Anglo-Indian man and the boy joined us.

"Can I help you?" asked the man, smiling.

"I'm wondering if I might go inside the church and have a look," I replied.

"Sure," he said, "let me get the key."

He reached into a little pouch formed by the knotted edge of his sarong, and pulled out a set of keys jiggling on a brass ring. "We have to keep the church locked now," he explained while looking for the appropriate key, "because there have been several burglaries. But on Sundays, the church is open all day." Having found what he was looking for, he unhooked it and gave it to the boy.

"Bring him in through the vestry," he said, patting the boy on the head.

"Is it all right with the priest?" I asked, intimidated by the dreadful possibility of accidentally surprising the priest while he was changing.

"I'm sure it's all right," said the man, in an authoritative tone. But I wanted more assurance.

Who was this bystander to presume to know what was acceptable to the priest and what was not?

"Is the priest around?" I asked.

"Of course," he replied.

"Can I meet him first?" I asked.

"Sure," he said, extending his hand, "I'm Father Alexander Kyaw Win."

I shook his hand hastily. I felt my cheeks burning and I knew the heat was not the cause. I felt I had to say something quick, so I began to explain how I got lost, but I soon found out it was not easy to make him—or anybody—understand why I had chosen to get lost deliberately. So I lied to the good father. And I would have kept on sinning if it weren't for the return of the boy, who came to tell me that the door to the vestry had been unlocked.

He led me to the chapel through the vestry. The sparseness of the vestry—a small dark room with nothing but a pair of gowns hanging meekly on the wall—made me think that either the father had been following the Franciscan ideal of simplicity to the point of self-denial or the two burglars had been extremely thorough. When we were seated next to each other on a pew in the chapel, an inquisition began; the boy asked where I was from, what I was doing in the city, why I was sitting in a small neighborhood church while the other tourists were climbing the steps of Shwe Dagon, and so on.

At one point, the Grand Inquisitor asked if I was a "Krishen." I told him I was not quite what he might call a Christian but an "Agnostic." The throaty Greek word, interjected in the middle of our Burmese conversation, had the effect of an anatomical reference in the middle of a royal banquet—it produced a shocking silence. Scowling suspiciously, the Grand Inquisitor demanded clarification. To explain the meaning of "Agnostic" in Burmese is truly a torture; my native tongue, whose origin is the canonical language of Buddhism, is so rich in expressions for acceptance and resignation, yet so inadequate when it comes to doubt and ambivalence. The greater the struggle to explain myself, the stronger the temptation to lie. I could have saved myself quite a bit of linguistic agony by telling him I was a "Krishen." I realized at that moment that the true purpose of an inquisition was not to uncover the truth—it was to make everything so difficult and unbearable for the accused that he or she finally broke down and confessed to the inquisitor's charges.

But I made it clear to my little Torquemada—and it wasn't easy—that I was neither denouncing nor embracing the Christian doctrine. Because I was neither a faithful nor a heretic, he didn't know whether to forgive me or condemn me. This is the cross all Agnostics must bear—no one knows exactly what to do with them. At best, they get a grudging dismissal, which was what I got from the boy.

I took his silence as my cue and began asking him questions for a change. "Well," he began, "I'm not from Rangoon," and he gave me the name and the description of the village where he was born. From his narrative, I judged it to be one of the fishing villages in the coastal area. "My parents died when I was very young, so I lived with my cousins. They weren't very nice." He wiggled his nose, as if he had just recalled something foul in his memory. "Did they hit you?" I asked. No answer. I began to form numerous theories about the limp that I had noticed earlier in his walk. But the boy's story had a happy ending. "I met Father Kyaw Win one day, and we became friends. I told him that I was unhappy, that I wanted to leave the village. My cousins—they were mean to me. So, he adopted me and brought me here."

There was a small piece of tapestry hanging from the edge of the table, held in place by nothing but a solitary brass cross. The Mother and the Holy Child, attended by a pair of cherubim, stared at us with the compassionate dark eyes characteristic of needlework icons. There was a mural of the crucifixion scene: Christ in a gold-colored loin cloth, Mary in a blue robe, Magdalene in a red shawl, and a mounted figure that looked very much like a knight in full armor with a raised lance, included by the artist either to give the Biblical scene a touch of heroism or to declare he or she could also do Medieval pastoral artworks. Though the style was recognizably Renaissance (El Greco tempered by Botticelli), the brilliance was unmistakably Burmese: the lush green meadows, the bright blue sky, and the purple clouds made Golgotha look more inviting than it should. Only Christian melancholy tempered by Burmese gaiety could produce such a delightful scene of suffering.

"Renovation?" I asked when I noticed a couple of bamboo ladders leaning on Christ's shoulders.

"Yes," confirmed the boy, "the colors are beginning to fade. It needs to be touched up."

By the time it was done, I thought, it might very well be the brightest crucifixion anyone would ever see.

When I came out, Father Kyaw Win was nowhere to be found. So I asked the boy to show me the easiest way to get back to Tamwe. The boy laughed out loud at my incredulity, and said, "This *is* Tamwe." Amazing! Suddenly, I was no longer lost. I showed him the address of my inn. He pointed to a building several blocks away that looked vaguely familiar to me, and said, "There's Workers' Hospital, so you can just . . ." I stopped him before he could suggest the exit behind the morgue. Everyone wanted me to go through this wretched dog hole for some reason. I asked for alternatives, but the boy couldn't think of any. I knew I had to be fairly close to the inn. It was a fine day, and the sun was bright, so I didn't want to rest—I wanted to follow all the way home what appeared to be the clues of a playful god. I decided to just walk in the general direction of Kandawgyi. The Indian man at the gate waved at me when our eyes met again for the last time.

As I turned the corner of the block, I heard loud laughter—the belly-rocking kind that could have only come from one who had stomached many of life's cruel jokes. I turned around, and saw Father Kyaw Win sitting inside a neighborhood watch-repair shop, sharing a cup of tea with the shopkeeper. Unlike the incongruous knight in the crucifixion scene, he blended into the background of his secular surrounding, even in his carnival-colored batik shirt. I couldn't picture him delivering a stern sermon wearing a stiff white collar, but I could easily picture him giving English lessons to the daughter of a meat merchant or sharing a bowl of fish-broth with a sidecar driver. We looked at each other through the shopkeeper's glass booth, where broken timepieces seemed to be singing a psalm in praise of eternity. "Thank you for stopping by," he shouted, waving his stalwart arm. Then he and the shopkeeper resumed their conversation, and I heard his laughter trailing behind me.

In Rangoon, everything is reduced in magnitude; the death of Christ is a colorful mural, and the death of a student who falls from a bus and gets run over by a car is a fairly typical traffic jam. It is easy to overlook the enormity of certain events and the greatness of certain individuals. The only way to see Rangoon in its true proportion is to see it through a pair of magnifying glasses. I like serendipitous discoveries because they give me a kind of reassurance. They prove the notion of destiny; they prove that whatever is lost by someone, is bound to be discovered by someone else. It is nice to know that nothing or no one can ever get lost completely. It gives me the courage to get lost and remain lost, until I feel I am ready to find the way home. Anyone can go into a Barnes & Noble and pick up a copy of Orwell's *Burmese Days*. But to find it the way I did— in a city an ocean away where saints still lived among the masses—is divine.

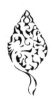

Tea Leaves
at Twelve

My friend Jonathan, one of the bravest gastronomic explorers I have ever encountered, marched into a Burmese restaurant in San Francisco with me one day and, without a flinch, conquered a plate of sour mango salad sprinkled with roasted chili seeds and a bowl of boneless chicken chunks buried underneath a pool of chili sauce. This undefeated tongue of his, which had successfully cut through India's turmeric sea and Hunan's ginger hill, came to a sudden halt when it accidentally fell into a swamp of pickled tea leaves, known in Burmese as *Lephet*. Horrified, he withdrew after his initial assault and refused to return to it. Seeing that he had abandoned this barbaric dish, I took full possession of it and, in a series of raids, cleared it of its native content.

The Buddhist principle of moderation is hardly ever observed in Burmese cooking. Burmese like to intensify the flavor of their dishes—they add chili powder to their peppery broth and fish sauce to their fried fish-cake salad. *Lephet* is traditionally served with a pot of hot tea, the result being a combination that guarantees insomnia not only with its caffeine content but also with recurring urinary urges. When I was studying for my matriculation exam, my mother made sure I was plentifully supplied with *Lephet*. Every time I headed for the kitchen with an empty plate, she intercepted me at the door to hand me a new plate. The routine was repeated with such exactitude that it began to resemble the cued exchanges between stage actors.

Every year, the matriculation exam, which was also known as the tenth-grade exam, drove thousands of Burmese students to a point approaching insanity, and a few to suicide. One could easily recognize those studying for the tenth-grade exam by their incoherent speech pattern (a symptom of sleep deprivation) and their garlic breath (evidence of excessive *Lephet* consumption). The Burmese education system did not look kindly upon independent thinking. Teachers were, in every sense of the word, dictators; instead of giving lectures or providing guidance, they dictated to their students a series of questions and answers. *What are the causes of the downfall of the first Burmese Empire? The causes of the downfall of the first Burmese Empire are . . . .*

There were recitation sessions, during which students were asked to recite from memory passages that had been dictated to them. Deviation of any kind from the original—be it a paraphrase or an omitted word—was considered a failed recitation. At the end of the session, those who had failed to recite the passages faultlessly were chastised before their classmates—with arms folded and facing the blackboard, they were caned one by one. The number of strikes a student received depended on the degree of inventiveness he or she had dared to exhibit—one strike for an omitted word, two strikes for an omitted phrase, but three strikes or more for substituting the original sentence with an entirely new one. I remember studying from dusk till dawn in my tenth grade, studying geometric shapes and geographic regions. *Lephet*, heavily garnished with chopped garlic and fried onions, dulled my palate, and the memorization incapacitated my reasoning. The weeks before the exam, I could not tell sugar from salt, nor could I differentiate an octagon from the continent of Europe.

Four months later, I heard on the radio that scores from the exam would be announced the following morning. Anxiety kept me awake the whole night. The next morning, I ran to the local college where the scores were posted. Glued on the mossy wall of the main building were sixty or seventy foolscap sheets containing typewritten names of those who had passed the exam. I also saw an impenetrable crowd— like a grotesque creature with countless heads and arms, and a belly that swelled and thinned as people moved in and out of it.

Taking advantage of a gap that appeared when someone tore himself away to redo his sarong that had become undone, I held my breath and dove into the crowd. Fumbling through ribcages and elbows, I resurfaced partially on the other side of the crowd, my head locked between two shoulders (of which neither was mine). My nose was two inches away from the names. But I was staring at names that began with the fifth alphabet. In order to find my name, which began with the last of the 33 Burmese alphabets, I needed to reposition my head. I sank back into the foul, dark womb of the crowd and once again began fumbling. The process had to be repeated numerous times before I found my name and was relieved to know that I had passed—my academic future had been guaranteed. Little did I know then that, five years later, my contemporaries and I would be prevented from graduating by political upheavals that eventually ended in bloodshed and massacre.

Lephet is as dark and bitter as the political history of Burma. I cannot eat it without thinking of the cloudy afternoon in August of 1988, when government troops opened fire on unarmed protesters. When the eyewitnesses later recounted how the sewers in downtown Rangoon ran red with blood that afternoon, they weren't being poetic. ("The Army aims straight, and it shoots to hit—it doesn't shoot aiming at the sky," gloated General Ne Win, Chairman of the Burmese Socialist Party at the time, in his national address televised on the same evening.) Hundreds of students, merchants, and monks were killed. Those who survived the bullets and bayonets were never the same. They lay awake at night, tormented by a kind of guilt similar to that which plane-crash survivors often felt—they repeatedly asked themselves, "Why were we spared?"

Martial law was declared in all major cities. There was a curfew from 6 P.M. to 6 A.M. We had to rush home before nightfall. We gathered around battery-operated transmitter radios, often in the darkness of a power outage, listening to BBC and Voice of America. Hope burned dimmer than the flickering candlelight. Anxiety, aided by a swarm of bloodthirsty mosquitoes, bit us everywhere. Through blinds and shutters, we saw truckloads of soldiers going from house to house, their footsteps awakening the empty city in sleep, and we knew many of our classmates who had actively participated in the demonstrations were being rounded up.

In the uneasy morning hours, when we met again in tea shops, we counted—with clenched fist and tight jaws—how many of us were spared the night before. We knew that few of those arrested would ever come home. In the meantime, Burmese Broadcasting Services televised romantic comedies and musicals as diversion. Because anger and guilt made us grind our teeth, we needed something to chew on. Because this was a test of our conviction and the answers to our moral questions had never been dictated to us before, we were on our own. We needed something to carry us through the darkest hours. *Lephet*, with an assortment of crushable nuts buried in its soft texture, was just the thing.

But *Lephet* did to me what conscience does to Macbeth and Lady Macbeth. Cawdor and his wife are haunted by what they have done. I, on the other hand, was reminded of what I believed I should have done but failed to do whenever I ate *Lephet*. My fascination with heroism was nothing but Quixotic fantasy. In reality, I had not the strength and the construct of a martyr. Therefore, during the uprising of 1988, I had limited my participation to that of a timid follower, leaving the roles of leaders to those with greater courage. But we were waging war, Gandhi-style, against totalitarianism.

The events that took place in Rangoon in 1988, by their sheer extraordinariness, rightfully demanded a certain degree of involvement from everyone who cherished freedom. Many of my contemporaries denounced the government publicly, made daring

speeches on raised podiums, and died on that afternoon when the troops opened fire on the crowd. I felt
the same outrage they felt, and I loathed the ruling
regime no less. But I did nothing beyond swelling the
procession now and again during rallies and echo-
ing the passionate cries of the protesters. What kept
me awake at night afterwards was the troubling
notion that I did too little; I could not help but feel
that I did less than what any decent man who found
himself in such a historic moment would have done.
I sometimes wished I were among those wounded
or arrested on that afternoon. But the moment had
passed, and I could not reclaim my martyrdom any
more than Cawdor and his wife could revive Duncan.

During my recent visit, riding around downtown
at night in a cab or in my uncle's car, I passed by
many pavement tea shops. "Look at this," said my
uncle, as he tried to negotiate a narrow street, half of
which was blocked by patrons spilling out of a tea
shop. "They should be arrested," said my uncle,
repeatedly pounding on the horn in exasperation to
clear the path ahead. A few of them eyed us with
disdain and grudgingly pulled themselves away to
let us pass. As we slowly drove by, I saw that the
side of our car actually came in contact with a few of
their hindquarters. Yet, amazingly, they continued to
puff their cheroots and drink their tea, hardly
acknowledging the fact that they could have easily
been knocked off their tiny stools and run over.

I recognized a kind of camaraderie in the dis-
missive manner in which they had chosen to shove
their buttocks in the face of danger. They were quite
typical of the young Burmese, mostly college and
university students, who spent a good portion of

their time discussing politics or poetry in sidewalk cafes and pavement tea shops. They sat around a single teapot and ate off the same plate of *Lephet*. They all carried Kachin satchels with similar tribal designs and they all had the sleeves of their white shirts rolled up to their elbows. Their heated debates flourished in the cool shade of a tarpaulin canopy, their brown faces lit by nothing but eagerness. There they sat, bordering on criminality day in and day out. Their disregard for law, much like the defiance of those who perished on that August afternoon in 1988, was a calculated attempt to undermine the authorities—it was, in short, a protest. A decade ago, a similar attitude of unanimous disobedience gave birth to a revolutionary movement. But these new rebels were a smarter breed. They were a nuisance but not a threat, so the Burmese army couldn't justifiably machine-gun them down. I felt like joining them for a spoonful of nostalgia no matter how bitter it might be.

Ten years ago, necessitated by the unsanitary conditions in which I was growing up, my body developed a kind of natural immunity against the germs and bacteria of Burma. My favorite noodle stall in Yang Kin district operated underneath a eucalyptus tree. Flies, attracted by the smell of fish sauce (which was impossible to distinguish from the smell of a sewer nearby), hovered above heaps of noodles like a swarm of locusts. The stall owner rinsed her hands and washed the dirty dishes in the same bucket of water. Everyone wiped his or her mouth on the same discolored rag dangling from a bamboo pole. I ate there regularly but somehow managed to ward off the malaria and cholera that came with every serving. But I had been so thoroughly cleansed by my Californian diet during the last ten years that I could not now drink water from a rustic faucet or eat food from a dusty kitchen in a third-world country without suffering some kind of bodily consequences. *Lephet* from a sidewalk establishment, where roaches were so domesticated they danced fearless in the warmth of the stove a few feet away from the patrons' feet, could be lethal.

"Here's my dilemma," I confessed to Sanda, my former classmate who was now an assistant lecturer, when I met her at U Chit Tea shop in Rangoon University's canteen. "I want to eat *Lephet*, but I've been abroad so long I'm not sure I can stomach something made in a tea shop or a café."

"Come visit me," she said. "I'll make you *Lephet*. And I'll invite over a few of our old friends so you can surprise them."

Her soft syllables and delicate features could be misleading. When we were in college, we both belonged to the half dozen unruly students whom most professors remembered as the primary cause of their headaches. She was, contrary to her demure mannerism, as resistant to discipline as the rest of us.

We hated Political Science lectures. The lecturer, in a monotonous tone devoid of conviction, dictated to us the glory of Socialism and the evil of Capitalism. Once, finding his lecture on "the class struggle between the oppressor and the oppressed" a bit too oppressive, we left through the back door and went to eat onion fritters near Inya Lake. We decided (democratically by an overwhelming majority of votes) that we would not attend any more Political Science lectures. But eventually we had to, when the semester reached its final quarter and we found we didn't have the foggiest idea what the "Burmese Way to Socialism" was. By then the lecturer had forgotten that we belonged to his class: "Are you sure you're in the right room?" he inquired, when we walked in to take our seats after a long absence.

My reunion with the gang took place at Sanda's house. After circling around in a maze of passages for fifteen minutes, my cab pulled into her front yard. From the garage and the porch emerged, preceded by loud shrieks, a number of familiar faces— Zin Ma, our unofficial group leader with a dignified smile, and Khin Oo, the pretty petite who had always been our quintessential Burmese rose. Khin Oo introduced me to her husband and her daughter. Curious, I asked how they met. Her modest husband described their encounter as "one of those upstairs-downstairs romances."

Romance between two complete strangers in Burma usually begins with the man giving the woman a note of some kind to declare his affection for her. The odds are so much against the success of such a romance, since he has to somehow deliver this note, discreetly, in spite of the watchful eyes of her protective siblings. I imagined Khin Oo's husband, this shy man before me, leaning on the edge of his veranda, nervously looking down, with a folded note in his hand. And I imagined Khin Oo suddenly appearing on the veranda below. Sensing his presence, she looked up, but she couldn't see who he was because the sun was in her eyes. Seizing the moment, he dropped the note. I pictured the thin piece of paper, carried away by playful summer breezes like a feather. I pictured him following the flight of his note with horrified eyes. His heart fluttered like a frightened butterfly. The note, which contained his private poetry, finally fell on the ground, resting quietly near the stairway to the apartment complex where he and Khin Oo both lived. He could only pray that it would not be discovered by Khin Oo's mother returning from the market. But somehow, at some point, my friend Khin Oo must have captured one of his floating notes and, along with it, his heart.

The preliminaries of the reunion over, we began gossiping and reminiscing about those who were missing. *So and so died in an automobile accident, and so and so is busy running a café he now owns.*

"Where's Bo Bo and Cho Ma?" I asked of a pair that used to be inseparable. Theirs was a budding friendship that blossomed into romance and eventually matured into matrimony.

Immediately, the smiles disappeared. I sensed reluctance and uneasiness around me. I realized, from the way our conversation sank into silence, that I had stirred up something they preferred to forget. I apologetically tried to steer the conversation back to a safe harbor. But Zin Ma decided to be forthcoming.

"Bo Bo is in prison," she said, pronouncing each word carefully so that the unpleasant truth need not be repeated for clarification.

"For what?" I asked blatantly, abandoning propriety altogether.

"He was first arrested for gambling," explained Zin Ma, "but later more charges were filed for his political activities."

Political activities? That didn't' sound like Bo Bo. He was from a wealthy merchant family. Politics was the last thing on his mind. He was interested in T-shirt designs and Ray-Ban models. He and two of his friends used to own a stall in Bogyoke Market. They sold primarily cosmetic products acquired through black marketeering—sneakers and denims from Thailand, Taiwan, or China that only sons and daughters of the affluent could afford. But Bo Bo was as much a customer to this business as he was a partner. If he and his friends were profiting, that profit came partially at Bo Bo's expense. I remember the time he was giving me a ride. He said he wanted to stop at the shop to take a look at a shipment of "elastic jeans" that had just arrived.

"Hey," he asked one of his friends behind the counter at the shop, "how much are we going to sell these for?" His friend quoted a price, which was half of what my father earned in a month working as an accounting supervisor for a government bank.

"Set this one aside for me," he said, pulling out a faded pair with frayed cuffs. "How much do I owe the store now?" he asked. His friend snatched a ledger and started tabulating. Apparently Bo Bo had a credit account of some sort that had to be reconciled with his share of the profit from the shop every month.

"Here," finally his friend produced the grand total. "That's what it'll come to if you add this one." Bo Bo chuckled to downplay the multiple-digit number on the ledger his friend was waving in his face.

I could think of many of my former classmates who had been actively involved in antigovernment activities during the uprising. I could even name a few who become guerrilla fighters after their bloody encounter with the government troops. Bo

Bo was never among them. If he had had any interest in politics, he had never expressed it in my presence. And that made it nearly impossible for me to understand how he, of all people, was put in jail for "political activities."

"So what happened to Cho Ma?" I asked.

"She's in Washington D.C.," answered Zin Ma.

I had more questions, but I could see that they had reached the limit of their frankness. They were too close to Bo Bo and Cho Ma, so a heavily edited version of the story was all they could manage.

The unexpurgated version of the story came to me the following evening, from two other former classmates who came to visit me at the inn. One gave me his business card, which read Energy Project Executive, Myanmar Daewoo Limited. I made a mental note to talk to him about the power outages. The other also gave me his card. It read Assistant Human Resource Manager, Myanmar Daewoo Limited, which partially explained how the first one was hired. Mine had my name and my contact information, followed in boldface type by the word *writer*—a haughty title I had no legitimate claim to since I had not yet published anything at the time. When they asked for my card, I said, "I didn't bring any."

I invested in two pints of scotch for each in order to increase the degree of frankness I could expect. The return on my investment was generous.

"They probably don't want to talk about this," began Ko Myint, "because what happened to Bo Bo was outrageous."

"It's a *dark* story," warned Myat Tun, who had always had a flair for melodrama. Perhaps, I suggested, they could shed some light on this *dark* story.

"It's true that Bo Bo was arrested first for gambling," explained Ko Myint. "He was arrested for Ché."

Ché is the practice of guessing and betting on the final digits of the wining ticket in Thai lottery. It is a common pastime activity in Burma, but it is also illegal. In Burma, legality or illegality of an act depends more on the whims of the government and less on the laws of the country. Black marketeering, though theoretically illegal, hasn't been prosecuted for so long that it is, at present, as good a trade as fishing or farming. But there's no guarantee that the government won't, at some point in the future, begin arresting black marketeers if it fears that the merchants are becoming too powerful and too influential a class.

"But," continued Ko Myint, "during the investigation, the army discovered that Bo Bo had been in communication with a group of activists who were posting anti-government literature on the Internet."

"I cannot imagine him playing a major role in this," I interjected.

"And he wasn't," responded Ko Myint. "He was not an organizer or a leader—nothing like that. At the most, he might have supplied some equipment or provided technical expertise. But it just happened that the government was vigorously going after unauthorized Internet users at the time. They were looking for someone or some group they could use as an example, and they found Bo Bo." I was reminded of a punch line from the Russian comedian Yakov

Smirnoff's standup routine: *In Russia, there's no such thing as a "warning shot"; they shoot you, and that's the warning for the next guy.* Bo Bo's arrest was the warning shot.

"I thought his father-in-law was a high-ranking military man," I said, remembering that Cho Ma was from an influential circle.

"Well," said Ko Myint," he still is. He's now in Washington D.C., serving as a diplomat of some sort, and doing quite well."

"So didn't he do anything when his son-in-law was arrested?" I asked. Ko Myint's jaw stiffened with indignation.

"You see," explained Ko Myint, "He *was* brought in when the investigation reached the crucial point. He could have intervened, and asked for some leniency from the authorities. But he was a couple of months away from a promotion at the time. So he chose instead to prove his loyalty to his superiors; he recommended the severest possible punishment for his son-in-law."

"So how exactly are things now between his wife and him?" I asked.

"What we heard," proceeded Ko Myint, after consulting Myat Tun, "was that his wife went to Ine Sein Jail and served him with divorce papers."

I remembered another time Bo Bo was giving me a ride home from school. He told his driver, a cheerful Bengali man, to park the car several yards away from a lecture hall and wait.

"I'm sorry," he said, "it'll just be a moment. Cho Ma's in this class. We'll leave as soon as she comes out."

"Are you giving her a ride too?" I asked.

"No," he said, "but I want to see her before I leave."

"Bo Bo, this is silly," I said, somewhat irritated that I was promised a ride but made to sit and wait. "You see her and talk to her every day."

"I know," he responded, "but I want to see her as much as possible." For the next thirty minutes or so, he sat motionless, staring intently at the door of the lecture hall through the windshield, waiting to catch a glimpse of her.

"Should I tell her how I truly feel about her?" he asked. It was a rhetorical question that needed no response. But I answered, prompted by impatience.

"Maybe you should tell her how you feel," I said, thinking the sooner it was over, the better it would be for all parties involved. Eventually he did, and so began the transformation of their relationship, from platonic to romantic, from friendship to courtship.

The U.S. State Department, in its Consular Information Sheet, warned me that Americans had in the past been "detained, arrested, tried and deported for, among other activities, distributing pro-democracy literature, photographing sites and activities, and visiting the homes and offices of Burmese pro-democracy leaders." Caroline Courtauld, in her guidebook to Burma, warned me that Burmese prisons were "best left unvisited." Every publication I brought along with me, in one section or another, warned that I should avoid politics like the plague while I was in Burma. But Bo Bo was not a prominent democratic leader; he was an ordinary man who, for a fairly ordinary offense, received an exemplary sentence due to unfavorable circumstances. Visiting a former classmate who was in jail, I reasoned, could hardly be deemed a political act. I kept picturing him in his small cell, staring at the tiles on the ceiling with the same stoicism with which he had once waited for Cho Ma to emerge from a lecture hall. Ten years ago, I failed to meet my political obligation to a country in her struggle against tyranny. I wasn't about to shy away from my moral obligation to a friend in misfortune.

"Where is he kept?" I asked.

"I heard that he was kept in Ine Sein Jail," said Ko Myint.

"But he was transferred to another place," interrupted Myat Tun.

No one could tell me with certainty where he was kept.

I met my friend Soe Myint again in the cafeteria of Bohosi Medical Center, where his mother was being hospitalized. He led me to a bench where, unbeknownst to me, a young couple had been awaiting my arrival.

"This is Tun Tun and Thida," introduced Soe Myint. I shook their sticky, moist hands. Tun Tun was an opulent, dark-skinned man in a striped T-shirt, and Thida a slim, fair-skinned woman in a long-sleeve blouse. They both looked extremely nervous; he kept twisting his fingers incessantly, and she kept avoiding my eyes.

"Go on," urged Soe Myint, "tell him your story." I had no idea what sort of story I was about to hear, but Tun Tun and Thida, the fidgeting principal characters, lent the narrative a Hitchcockean suspense mode before it even began. And the fact that I was invited to hear it could only mean one thing—they wanted me to play a part of some importance.

"We are lottery winners," Tun Tun began his befuddling prologue. Perhaps this was a happy story. "We won the visa lottery," he added, a few seconds after I congratulated him. I had to turn to Soe Myint for some explanatory footnotes. Apparently, the number of immigration applications the American Embassy received in Burma far exceeded the quota of immigrants allowed. So the embassy resorted to a kind of lottery system to determine who among those thousands of applicants would receive their visas. Tun Tun and Thida, clarified Soe Myint, were among the lucky few (ten or eleven thousand) who had been promised visas. But as it turned out, the winners in this lottery were not much better off than those in Shirley Jackson's short story; they would now have to run a bureaucratic gauntlet, in which they were hit at every turn with one kind of demand or another by corrupt officials.

"So," continued Tun Tun, "first we'll have to prove that we can get work to support ourselves in America; we can furnish the embassy with our high school diplomas, college degrees, and employment records. Then, we'll also need a sponsor—someone who'll temporarily put us up when we first arrive in America."

At some point during this monologue, I began searching for a way to tell him I was hardly a suitable choice for a sponsor. But that, to my relief, was not the role they had in mind for me.

"We have no problem with any of these," resumed Tun Tun. "The problem is, we don't speak English that well, and we have no time to go to all those different offices. Half the time, we don't even know what we need or where to go. So we retained a *Pwe Sar*."

The Pwe Sar, an agent who agreed to represent them for a fee, promised them that, for 100,000 kyats (about $285 at the exchange rate at the time), he would assume responsibility for everything, up to the moment of their interview with the American consular. The 100,000 kyats, Soe Myint inserted, did not include bribes the couple had to pay various government agencies to obtain the documents needed—it was strictly the Pwe Sar's fee.

Burmese bureaucracy is like a prostitution ring—every favor has a price. The paper-pushing clerk at the bottom skillfully withholds, delays, and releases the incoming application according to the type of gift he or she receives. The pen-squeezing officer at the top doesn't give one the satisfaction of his or her signature unless he or she receives something of monetary value in return. In between, administrators with varying degrees of authority subject the sweating applicant to pleasure and pain alternately: "We'll be discussing your case this week," teases one; "we don't know what happened to your paperwork," frightens another.

A Pwe Sar is a professional hustler hired by an applicant who is too embarrassed to engage in those bureaucratic maneuvers. By the time the whole process is over, the applicant, who has to financially satisfy the Pwe Sar as well as the bureaucrats, is left drained and exhausted, financially, mentally, emotionally. I noticed my narrator's humble attire—the discolored stripes on his shirt, the frayed edge of his sarong, and the patched-up rubber sandals.

"We thought it was well worth the headaches and the troubles we were saving ourselves—we could rely on him to make sure that our paperwork was submitted on time."

The paperwork was eventually returned unprocessed by the embassy. Tun Tun, as if he was presenting me with a sacred document, cordially handed me with both hands a Xeroxed copy of what was returned. I observed that the Pwe Sar, for some unexplainable reason, did not complete several sections clearly marked "mandatory." "We are unable to process your visa applications," informed the note from the embassy, "due to incomplete information . . . ." The helpful embassy staff highlighted *and* circled the word "mandatory" with a thick blue marker. So what, I inquired, did the Pwe Sar do to remedy the situation?

"He did help us resubmit the completed applications," answered Tun Tun, his right hand squeezing his left as if it were the imaginary neck of the incompetent Pwe Sar, "but that was four or five months ago. Now, we are noticing that some of the winners who submitted their applications after we did have already received their visas. So we're worried—we're thinking our applications might have missed the deadline because of the delay. We tried to contact the Pwe Sar, but he wouldn't respond to us anymore."

"We're tired of wondering," added Thida wearily. "We just want a resolution, one way or another." Hope, for those who had to nurture it without any certainty, could be quite a strain. During the intermission, while the narrative was suspended, the hero and the heroine exchanged glances. And in those glances I saw the poignant picture of a couple that was, for better or worse, determined to win or lose together, each borrowing strength and consolation from the other.

Enter an American on vacation!

"That's where we need your help," said Soe Myint, the director who had brought this cast together. I held my breath as he prepared to define my role. "We're hoping you can call up your embassy," *my* embassy? " . . . and verify the status of their visas."

"You know," I cautioned them, "I'm just an ordinary tourist." Did they think I was someone influential from the foreign office?

"But," they reminded me, "you're an *American* tourist." They thought *all* Americans were influential. This was the curse of The Lone Ranger and Indiana Jones. Too strong is the myth of the American hero who arrives on horseback to save the natives that all American tourists are doomed to live up to it. It didn't help that I, compelled by my sympathy for the leading man and lady, decided rather to strut and fret my hour on stage than tell the director that I was wrong for the part.

The next morning, before I went to see my old classmates in Rangoon University, I phoned the embassy under the pretext that I was notifying it with my arrival as the State Department had recommended all Americans should; in doing so, explained the consular information sheet, we ensured that the embassy knew how to contact us if there was an emergency and we needed to be airlifted to safety. After I had provided the clerk with all the information, I addressed the case of the unlucky lottery winners.

"By the way *Nyi Ma Lay* (little sister)," I began, feigning familiarity, "I promised my friends I would also check on the status of their visas. Can you help me?" Then I gave her the seven-digit case-number assigned to Tun Tun and Thida. The clerk, a young Burmese girl with a nasal voice, was clearly untouched by my appeal.

"Well," she answered, "I can't—I'm busy now. Can you have your friends call me directly this afternoon?" Perhaps this was not going to be as difficult as everyone had made it out to be, I thought. I requested her name and her extension, which she surrendered somewhat unwillingly.

While returning from Rangoon University, the cab Soe Myint and I were sharing blew a tire on a road that was, by sheer coincidence, a few blocks away from Tun Tun's flat. When asked how long it might take to replace the flattened tire, the cab driver, veiled in a thick film of fume and ambiguity, shrugged.

"Why don't you wait over there," he suggested, pointing at a tea shop nearby. "Get yourselves something to drink, and I'll come get you when I'm done."

"We'll wait up there," said Soe Myint, pointing at the veranda of the two-story house where Tun Tun lived. "Just drive up to that house and holler when you're done."

When we knocked, Tun Tun came to the door, rubbing his eyes. We had obviously interrupted his afternoon nap. I told him about my phone call to the embassy and gave him the piece of paper on which I had written down the clerk's name and extension. His eyes widened. Extending his hands in a reverential manner, he accepted the paper. Then he rapidly waddled away to use his neighbor's phone. Tun Tun's mother, seated on a sedan in a corner, stared at the clear blue sky beyond the window with watery eyes as I went on an unguided tour of the flat. There were monotone photographs hanging on the wall, all enlarged and framed—a young man in army uniform looking at the camera apprehensively; a wedding picture encircled within a wreath; a much older couple, holding each other tenderly against the backdrop of a pagoda; a younger version of Tun Tun in graduation gown; and many more which revealed the crucial moments in the saga of this family.

I considered what Tun Tun's departure might mean to his silver-haired mother, whose metamorphosis from a prim young girl to a dignified family matriarch I had just witnessed in the photographic chronicles mounted on the wall. A permanent fixture near the door, she would sit day in and day out waiting for the postman to arrive with a letter from her son in America. Her eyes too weak and her hands too shaky to hold anything firmly, she would have her younger son read her the letter. Then, eventually, her younger son, inspired by his brother's description of Los Angeles and Hollywood, would tell her that he too wished to go to America. Each month, she would receive a modest sum of money from her two sons, who would go to great length to conceal the fact that they were struggling as underpaid auto mechanics, sharing a tiny apartment. The Polaroid shots of her sons at Disneyland (next to a gigantic Mickey Mouse) would not be large enough to make a graceful supplement to the photographic chapters of family history. When the old photos had faded beyond recognition, the wall would be emptier than ever.

Tun Tun returned, looking frustrated.

"How did it go?" I inquired.

"Not good," he answered. "She didn't pick up the phone. I think she can tell who's calling. She doesn't want to talk to me."

"How can she tell who's calling?" I asked, perplexed.

"They have those phones in the embassy that show who's calling," he answered.

"But you were using your neighbor's phone," I said.

"Yes," he clarified, "but the number is associated with our applications—I have inquired about it from this phone before, so she can tell the call is from one of the applicants." Caller ID as deterrence against those who attempted to bypass proper procedures—the embassy was certainly putting technology to good use.

We heard the cab driver's screechy voice at that moment. While we were walking back to the cab, Tun Tun and Soe Myint discussed my role.

"Can you ask him to go to the embassy and talk to the consular tomorrow?"

"Well, I'll talk to him about that."

"Can you also ask him to follow up with the Immigration Office back in America when he gets back home?"

"Yes, yes."

"I feel bad asking him for help, but we're pretty desperate, as you can see."

"I know, don't worry."

The conversation went on for a while in my presence. Several days ago, while visiting Sule Pagoda, I overheard an old lady muttering to herself as she sulkily placed flowers in the shrine of a deity:

"This is utterly useless," she said under her breath, " . . . it has done nothing for me . . . why I even bother with these flowers, I don't know . . . ." She was, I later discovered, voicing her dissatisfaction with the deity that had apparently failed to bring to fruition her wishes. When asked why she wouldn't be more forthcoming with her disappointment, she replied, "I might offend it." In other words, her whispers of dissatisfaction were meant to be heard—they were her grudging prayers. She wouldn't directly confront the deity because she didn't want to risk offending this deity. Evidently, some kind of relationship with this supernatural being, however dysfunctional, was better than no relationship with it at all. It was with a similar kind of shrewdness that my companions were pleading with me indirectly; they didn't want pester me, so they talked among themselves in a way that would allow me to over-hear their exchange.

"What are you doing tomorrow morning?" asked Soe Myint once we were back in the cab. Earlier, while he was conversing with Tun Tun, I had a chance to contemplate the weight of the responsibility I was naïvely accepting; so much was at stake for this couple. I had been miscast for the part from the start—I was hardly suited for the omnipotent role I was chosen to play.

"Soe Myint," I said apologetically, "I want to help your friends, but I cannot." I pointed out to him that I was not their legal counselor; I should not be speaking or acting on their behalf. I also explained to him that the embassy staff wouldn't appreciate a tourist interfering with its operations. Like the old lady at the pagoda, he refrained from expressing to me directly his disappointment, but I could read it in his frown. I felt like a deity who had failed its devoted worshippers.

A few nights afterwards, driven by uneasiness, I went out in search of diversion and in the process I met Thet Thet. If one is plagued by boredom at eleven at night in Rangoon, one has very few options for amusement—one can saunter through downtown's carnival-like night-market that stretches along Sule Pagoda Road, to examine piles of Seiko and Omega watches and Zippo lighters (their price so low and their quantity so great that one cannot help but wonder if they have been domestically assembled in the attic or garage of an enterprising Burmese family), or one can visit some of the nightclubs scattered across the city. I chose the latter.

The hostess handed me a coupon, with the silhouette of a naked African warrior holding a grinning shield that barely covered his private parts. The flyer read "Zulu Night." I hesitated before the staircase spiraling down into the darkness. I didn't want to be the dressy missionary in the middle of a hundred natives dancing naked—they would eat me alive. But Zulu Night, I later learned from the hostess, was the next evening. Relieved, I headed downstairs.

When I mentioned the name of the club during breakfast the following morning, I was told it was "classier" than the one near the fruit and vegetable market; "the girls there wait for you to make the first move," someone noted. Apparently that was how he defined "classy." But Thet Thet did not wait— she approached me first.

She hopped onto the stool next to mine and introduced herself to me. The tight long-sleeved batik dress with floral prints, which lent her the elegance of a courtesan painted on a lacquer bowl, was at odds with the candy-sucking Lolita that she was trying to play. Once pleasantries were exchanged, she thrust her face before my nose to show me the swelling on her cheek, as if she was asking me to smell her fragrance or admire her earrings. I asked her how she got injured.

"My dad hit me," she replied nonchalantly. Her indifference gave me a jolt. I had her repeat it to make sure I heard her correctly. The impact of the fist was still visible as a bluish stamp on her tender skin.

"Why did he hit you?" I asked.

"Well," she explained, rubbing her cheek and sticking her tongue out in a comical manner, "people say stuff about me—you know—neighbors. He hears them call me a slut, a whore, and he sometimes sees me coming home late, dropped off by different men in cars. He is old-fashioned—retired army man. He gets embarrassed, I guess. I don't think he knows what I do exactly, but I'm sure he suspects something. So, the other day, when I came home in the morning—at about three—he was waiting for me in the living room." I didn't need to hear anymore; I told her I could guess the rest. And the vision of a grown man slapping his own daughter with the hand that used to carry a rifle was not a pretty one.

"And what exactly *do* you do?" I probed.

"When people visit an exotic country," she launched her analogy, "they try out some of the local delicacies, right?" Right, I agreed, somewhat hesitantly—I could predict where this was heading.

"Well," she continued, throwing her hands in the air to show me the girls loitering around the bar, "think of them—of us—as local delicacies. It'll be a shame if someone comes all the way here, from Japan or America or wherever, and goes back without even sampling a local dish. That's not right—he should try it—at least to find out what it tastes like." Suddenly, I had a craving for pickled tea leaves.

"Why do you do this?" I asked.

"My dad doesn't go out much," she remarked, dropping her voice as if she was afraid someone might overhear her. "He's kinda simple-minded. He doesn't realize that we cannot afford to keep my brother in school if it weren't for my income. Of course, I'd prefer to be doing something else, but this is easy money, and I want my brother to stay in school. I love him—we have only each other." She frequently shrugged her shoulders playfully, but the burden on those shoulders, I realized, was no plaything.

"How much do you charge?" I asked.

"Fifteen to twenty thousands for a night," she said, brightened by the thought that she had found a client. I began converting her numbers in my head—15,000 to 20,000 kyats was about 45 to 60 dollars. This was affordable to me. An idea began to form in my head.

Sitting a few inches away from her, I began to see this little hair-tossing eye-rolling nymph for more than what she was. She was, I mused, a make-up test for all the ones I had previously failed. Here, finally, was someone I could save—a humanistic obligation I could meet.

"Here," I said, thrusting several $20 bills into her hand, "take it, and go home."

"For what?" she asked, perplexed.

"Just take it," I said. "Take the night off and spend some time with your brother."

"No, no," she said, flustered, "that's not right—I should do something for you."

I told her I didn't expect anything from her. She insisted that she be allowed to do something for me in return; she didn't believe in taking something for nothing. That was admirable, but I was trying to perform a redemptive act of charity; so I needed her to accept something for nothing. The lottery-winner couple I met earlier, my friend in captivity, and my classmates who had been shot and killed a decade ago—I owed them something. I had to settle my debt. Paying off Thet Thet was, in a sense, my attempt to settle a debt for less than what I actually owed—I was cheating.

"I really feel like I should do something to earn this," she said, as she rolled and unrolled the bills. I decided I would try a local dish—not the sanitized version foreigners sampled in fancy restaurants but the raw, untamed, authentic version the natives ate off curbside establishments.

"Maybe you can come have *Lephet* with me," I suggested.

"But it's midnight," she said; "there aren't too many places still open." She meant there weren't too many upscale restaurants open this late.

"There ought to be some pavement tea shops," I ventured.

"I know of one or two," she said, "but are you sure you want to do this?"

"Sure," I said, feeling invincible.

We went to a tea shop on Latha Road (Moonshine Road), and found a table underneath a flickering streetlight. I sat on a small stool the size of a cereal box, precariously balanced on it like a circus-bear on a unicycle. The shopkeeper came out and wiped the table with a discolored rag, whereupon the tabletop, covered in a thick coat of grease and dust, shone like polished mahogany. I constantly moved my feet to avoid cramps as well as to avoid what looked like a red-ant colony.

Thet Thet placed an order of *Lephet*. It came, garnished with six or seven pieces of green chilies, in a tiny tin plate. As if to prevent us from swallowing too much too fast, we were each provided with no utensil other than a spoon the size of a dime. Thet Thet mixed the dark leaves with small piles of peanuts and fried beans before pronouncing it ready for consumption. But before I had swallowed my first mouthful, Thet Thet interrupted me.

"Take a look at this," she said, swinging a plastic key-holder before my eyes like a hypnotist. I took it into my hand to observe it closer. The ring looked unfinished; it seemed to have been haphazardly cut. The hook was not secure; it was unfastened by a light squeeze, releasing the keys into my lap.

"My brother is manufacturing and marketing these," said Thet Thet, "and they sell really well, so if you want to invest in something here—in Burma— you should come talk to him."

I scrutinized the item again to ensure that I had not overlooked a revolutionary invention. I had not; it was just an ordinary key-holder and, judging from its performance during my quality inspection earlier, it was not exactly the model everyone would be rushing out to get. Not knowing what to say, I commented on its color (neon yellow): "It stands out, so it won't get lost easily," I said.

"Your brother should talk to investors and entrepreneurs," I added. But I omitted to tell her that her brother should also find a better manufacturing plant. "I'm just a sightseer," I reminded her, as I handed her back the prototype. She accepted it sullenly. She watched me quietly as I ate the cold, bitter pile of tea leaves.

Afterwards, we shared a cab to our respective destinations—I to my inn and she to her home. She was deep in contemplation. She turned to me occasionally, as if she were about to ask me something, but she never did, until the cab pulled up in front of the inn and I prepared to leave.

"I'm going on a trip next week," she said. "A pilgrimage to Kyaik Htiyo." She was referring to a tiny pagoda perched on a huge boulder on a cliff in Moulmein District (where Orwell, according to his famous autobiographical essay, shot an elephant). The pilgrimage, if it is still as it was ten years ago, is a physically punishing one; pilgrims have to follow a crude, narrow path winding up and down several hills, without the safety and comfort of handrails. The real attraction is not the pagoda, but the boulder, which perilously rests on the edge of a steep cliff in a manner that defies laws of gravity and physics.

"Can you give me some money for the trip?" she asked. Was she asking me to sponsor her pilgrimage? Was she selling me absolution? She could not have correctly guessed the perverse motivation behind my philanthropy earlier in the evening, but she seemed to have realized that I was getting away with something. If she was too proud to take something for nothing, she was also shrewd enough to know when she was giving away too much for too little. $40 was too small a price for the sort of full-scale redemption I sought—she wanted more.

But I had no more; after paying the cab driver, I had but $5 left in my wallet. I handed her the remaining small bills. She looked at these and then at me with disappointment. I hastily walked into my room without looking back, filled with anger, shame, and guilt, realizing I had once again been cheated out of an opportunity to redeem myself. The repugnant taste of tea leaves lingered in my mouth, like the smell of rotten flowers left on the altar of an incompetent deity by dissatisfied worshippers.

The Marionettes of Bogyoke Market

"Here comes a foreigner," alerted the owner of the outermost stall, which seemed to serve as a sentry post, when I approached an aisle. Awakened, those from the neighboring stalls, who had been reposing in different states of abandon, hastily rose to reclaim modesty by buttoning their opened blouses and straightening their crumpled sarongs, like officers scurrying back to their posts at the sound of a bugle. Panic began. Shouts in Burmese flew back and forth.

"Where's Kyaw Oo?"

"We need Kyaw Oo—does any one know where he is?"

"He told me he was going to have lunch."

"You know where he eats?"

"He usually eats at the noodle stalls."

"Someone go fetch him—*you* go fetch him."

"But he might be somewhere else."

"Then find him!"

"Tell him a foreigner just walked in and we need him."

"Hurry!"

Having received his order, an errand boy shot off in the direction of the food stalls to find Mr. Kyaw Oo, presumably the only merchant in the aisle who spoke English with communicable fluency. His service, therefore, was desperately needed, for his neighbors had been badly surprised by my unanticipated arrival. They pined for his return, watching the entrance the way a besieged army would scan the horizon for reinforcement. I considered saying something in Burmese to ease their anxiety, but I changed my mind. With these Burmese merchants in Bogyoke Market as a defending army, myself as a solitary foreign invader, and the errand boy as the Paul Revere who was already halfway between Boston and Lexington, the drama was unfolding too fast for me to put an end to it. So I decided to play along.

Half a dozen pairs of eyes were trained on me; no movement of mine, however minute, escaped their notice. Whenever I paused to admire something, they barraged me with a variety of offers. When I threw a glance at a satchel, they threw half a dozen in different designs over my head, lassoing me with shoulder straps. When I reached for a sarong, they draped me in scores of patterns. And if I, out of curiosity for the merchandise or sympathy for the merchant, consented to try on something, I was instantly hauled into a secluded corner (which was apparently reserved as the fitting-area because of its scarce foot-traffic) to be mummified in a complete set of ceremonial costumes—a silk turban, a lapel-less linen coat, and an elaborate sarong woven by hand in threads of silk and gold.

"No, no, he's light skinned—that tan color won't do."

"Well, what do you suggest?"

"Here, put this one on."

"Robin egg?"

"Yes, the darker tone suits him better."

"Look, this is not good material—give me back the other one."

"Just put that one on and let me see how he looks in it."

So began a tug of war between the two opinionated assistants of a merchant determined to put together an ensemble for me, pronto. They couldn't agree on a color scheme for me, so they both dressed and undressed me simultaneously, each after a fashion. When I tried to leave, they hastily unfolded a roll of fabric and held it before me, as if they were fishermen with a net and I, a fat catfish slithering away. The owner of the adjacent stall, who had been watching us in silence, beckoned me with a wave, teaching me with bodily gestures how I might escape my captors. I fled to his stall, slipping past the net from below as he had indicated, and he received me with a burst of laughter.

Between the stalls of Bogyoke Market, there appeared to be invisible boundaries of commerce. Never did two merchants trade with me at once; they traded with me one at a time. When I was in the vicinity of one stall, no merchant other than the one who owned the stall would address me. Only after I had crossed the invisible boundary would another merchant begin offering me his or her merchandise. Their communal respect for territorial boundaries convinced me that there was solidarity among them; this native army, I thought, would not be easily thrown into disarray, for there was discipline among its rank and file.

Bogyoke Aung San Market, or General Aung San Market, was formerly Scott Market. It was later renamed in honor of the national hero who began a series of military and diplomatic efforts that eventually led to Burma's independence from Britain in January 1948. Doomed to martyrdom like most revolutionary heroes, he was gunned down on a rainy day six months later, along with his bodyguard and his cabinet members, while drafting a new constitution. In his ubiquitous monotone photo, which graces the hallways of schools and the walls of government buildings, he wears a broad-collared overcoat and an officer's cap that seems one size too big for his delicate head; but partially exposed beneath the militant shadow of his cap is a youthful officer with an idealistic gaze, his boyish smile framed within a chiseled jaw-line.

At the high school I attended, there was, and probably still is, an annual essay contest held in honor of the General. A few of us, notable aspiring writers, were regularly invited to participate. Should there be an insufficient number of voluntary participants, those who had ignored their invitations were asked to sign up: "Participation is voluntary, but you *must* participate," ruled our teacher. On the appointed afternoon, we were cloistered in a stifling corner for a period of two to three hours, our quietude unmarred by such mundane distractions as the sight and sound of our friends in the canteen or on the soccer field. The *punkas*, the old-fashioned ceiling fans, were operable only when essential elements such as switches, wires, and electricity were all in peak condition. On rare occasions, when all the requirements were met, those suspended beasts flapped their wings, first with the methodical sluggishness of someone awakening from a lengthy coma, and later with the agonizing whines of someone stretching his or her stiffened joints. As they spun faster, the organic deposits (cakes of dust, pieces of cobwebs, and dead spiders) sitting undisturbed on their wings became loosened and fell upon us in chunks of various sizes.

Sweating profusely, with smoking fans a few feet above our heads, we were asked to list the achievements of General Aung San, the Father of Burmese Independence. Since we were merely reproducing, with little or no modification, the standardized biography of the General in our textbooks, the variety of essays was nowhere near the variety of merchandise in the General's market. We wrote how the colonial government, adopting the "divide and rule" policy, created dissension among ethnic tribes in Burma by favoring some and ignoring others; and we wrote how the General, equipped with nothing but sheer determination, traveled across the country to persuade the tribal leaders to sign a peace treaty, named *Pin Lone Treaty* after the city of Pin Lone in Shan State where it was signed.

"Where's he from?"

"Don't know; he hasn't said a word."

"Japanese, I think."

"Japanese are rich."

"Of course they are."

"He's coming your way. Be sure to quote the highest price!"

"Oh, I will, I will. Just make sure you do the same when he comes to you!"

The unity of the merchants in the General's market was founded upon their common desire to exploit me as a collective body; therefore, any merchant who was willing to dishonor their impromptu price agreement and undersell was a threat to the collective. As I moved from stall to stall, I noticed that each merchant, risking the wrath of his or her neighbors, was trying his or her best to keep me from moving on. United by a common cause yet divided by their individual ambitions, this army of merchants resembled the warring ethnic tribes, whose leaders General Aung San had had much trouble bringing together under the same roof.

Mr. Kyaw Oo, the relief everyone had been anxiously awaiting, finally appeared with the young footman who was sent to summon him. The merchants lost no time in bringing him to me; panting and protesting, he was thrust before me. Still wiping beads of sweat off his forehead with the edge of his sarong, which had been fastened high above his knees lest it should impede his marathon from the noodle stall to the souvenir stall, he faced me, his foreign foe, with the confounded expression of a gladiator who had been thrown into the arena before he had had a chance to properly prepare for his encounter with the exotic beast.

"Are you sure he speaks English?" asked the doubtful champion, examining his opponent's oriental features.

"He looks Japanese," observed a spectator timidly.

"Well, I don't speak Japanese," said the champion, trying to retreat to a safe distance. But the crowd was eager for combat; they pushed him back before me.

"Just talk to him—Japanese speak English too," urged an impatient spectator.

"It's hard to understand them when they speak English," said the reluctant champion. "I won't understand his accent." Then he reminded the crowd of an embarrassing episode from the past: *"Remember* what happened the last time a Japanese came?"

He was undoubtedly referring to a time when he, equally ill-equipped, engaged a busload of Japanese tourists in conversation with disastrous results. But the bloodthirsty crowd refused to relent; they pushed him back into the arena. The champion seemed so genuinely demoralized that I—his opponent, the foreign creature—found it necessary to reassure him everything was going to be fine.

"How are you?" I greeted him in English.

"Fine," he responded with relief, "and how are you?"

We were before a stall that sold statuettes and marionettes. The stall owner, whose glazed brown skin was the color of varnished wood, was drinking tea from a small saucer; seated cross-legged, he blew on the steaming content and swallowed it, slurping noisily, with the haughtiness of a baron. When he saw me trying to disentangle a marionette hanging from a pole, he abandoned his decorum and hastened to my assistance.

"Come on," he invited the interpreter, "tell him what they are—give him some historical background."

"What historical background?" asked the interpreter.

"How they came to be, and all that," said the stall owner.

"But I don't know how they came to be, " said the interpreter.

"Then explain to him what they are," suggested the stall owner.

"All right," agreed the interpreter, taking a deep breath and clearing his throat in preparation for the great undertaking ahead.

I waited. Soon, in an air of scholasticism, and in a commingling of English and Burmese that was a language in its own right, he began discharging his duty.

"These are *Barmees* puppets," he prefaced. "This one is the prince," he introduced one in a silver dress and a turban. "We call it *mintha* in *Barmees*, . . . he is the hero, always happy, always smiling, . . . he lives in the *nandaw*, that is to say, he lives in the . . . the . . . palace." He encouraged me to examine closely the permanent smile painted on the prince's face. "And this one," he introduced another in a long silk dress with raven hair, "we call it *minthami*, she is the princess . . . she is the *lady-hero*, happy and smiling, she lives in the *nandaw* with the *mintha* . . . in *Barmees* stories, they make love with each other, and they dance together." To illustrate the romance between the prince and the princess, he placed the two marionettes side by side and shook them simultaneously. The spasmodic duet of the *mintha* and the *minthami* abruptly came to an end when, due to their ill-choreographed twitches and bounces, their strings became inextricably entangled.

"This is *wungyi*," he introduced the next one, which wore an oblong headdress and a black gown, "he is the . . . the minister . . . he gives the king advice, sometimes he gives bad advice." Everyone got the joke—they laughed. Emboldened by the success of his comic debut, he continued, forcing the puppet to perform a solo number for me by swinging it before my face. "The *wungyi* lives in the *nandaw* too, with the *mintha* and the *minthami*." Naturally. Thankfully, I was spared the trio dance—the scandalous threesome involving the prince, the princess, and the minister—because the stall owner was unable to free the royal couple from the strings that bound them together.

The next one he chose was carved in dark wood. It wore a chuckle between a pair of sharp fangs, and a showy velvet coat of betel-juice red. "This is the *belu*," he introduced it in a tone of exaggerated alarm, feigning terror with bulging eyeballs; he was trying to warn me that it was a creature of fear and loathing. "The *belu* is a . . . a kind of a . . . ." His speech came to a halt; he had yet to find the proper terminology for this creature that was neither of a happy disposition nor from the *nandaw*-dwelling family.

An emergency meeting went into session; the interpreter, the stall owner, and a few bystanders met in a corner to discuss the attributes of the *belu*. Someone suggested "ghost" as the English equivalence of *belu* but he was immediately voted down: "A ghost is the spirit of a dead person," clarified someone, "but the *belu* has very little to do with death." Another suggested "monster" but she too met with numerous objections.

"A demon perhaps," I ventured. They looked at the wicked smile on the puppet's face. They looked at one another. They mauled over my proposal, and adopted it, with an amendment—a *belu*, they conceded, was a "*Barmees* demon."

A *belu* is a mythological creature, an antagonist or a villain, that frequently appears in Burmese epics. In the localized version of the Indian epic *Ramayana*, a poetic account of the great battles between the fair-skinned Aryans of northern India and the dark-skinned Dravidians of southern India, the demonic king of Sri Lanka is depicted as a *belu*. Doomed to play one sinister role after another, its marionette counterpart is traditionally painted black or blue, wearing an ostentatious headdress, and an expression that is somewhere between mockery and fury. Its dance, unlike that of the jovial *mintha* and *minthami*, is always menacing and its footfalls always syncopated with the threatening thuds from the drum.

Burmese marionettes come in a finite variety of archetypes: heroes, heroines, villains, and a cast of minor characters, such as monsters, sorcerers, sages, and buffoons. Burmese marionette theater, just like Burmese live theater, is heavily influenced by Buddhism. Since the memoir of Siddhartha Gautama is a portion of the canonical text for Burma's Buddhist audience and an inexhaustible source of royalty-free material for Burmese dramatists, the theatrical amusement for any given evening is likely to include episodes from the countless previous lives of Gautama. If the puppeteer has chosen an incredibly lengthy saga that requires several installments to conclude, the drama can stretch beyond one evening, to the delight of the playgoers; one famous tragedy based on Gautama's previous life as an elephant king includes a flashback of yet another previous life of his, making the unabridged presentation of this saga a drama that stretches across several nights *and* several lifetimes.

Just as Gautama, on his path to enlightenment, has to endure many torturous incarnations, each one being that of a virtuous individual under trying circumstances, so does each marionette cycle through a number of tragic or comic roles: if, for instance, *The Enlightenment of Prince Teza* (the tale of Gautama's incarnation as a prince) is on the bill for one evening and *The Court of Mahor Thada* (the tale of Gautama's incarnation as a Solomon-like judge) is on the bill for the following evening, the same *mintha*-puppet and *minthami*-puppet are likely to play Prince Teza and his betrothed on the first night, and Judge Mahor Thada and his wife on the second with no difference in appearance, save some minor changes in their costumes. And nothing is as comedic and as tragic as a virtuous Buddhist puppet in unfortunate circumstances—bouncing between human despair and religious epiphany, it sings its lament in a husky voice (for such is the vocal quality of most Burmese puppeteers, who are themselves lamenting the imminent death of their noble art).

"Look! I think he's going for the *belu*."

"I know, I know—he seems quite fascinated by it."

"How much are you going to ask for it?"

"Six dollars."

"Wow! That's cruel."

"Well, I'm sure he'll bargain, so I'll probably get four or five dollars in the end."

"Yes, but that's still quite a bit—these are sold for about two dollars each."

"But he looks like he can spare more than that."

It seemed I had been chosen to play the gullible foreigner for the amusement of these merchants. Overhearing them conspiring against me in Burmese, which they never suspected I understood, I couldn't help but be reminded of Shakespearean villains who hiss and whisper their inner thoughts, their schemes and plots against their opponents, for the benefit of the audience. These merchants, like their Elizabethan dramatic counterparts, spoke words that were never meant to be heard, yet they were heard loud and clear. There was a little bit of Shylock in each of these stall owners.

The scene also happened to be one that I had rehearsed and performed numerous times, so I knew my cues and lines by heart. Whether the locale is Rangoon, Bangkok, Jakarta, or Venice, the scene is always the same. The gullible foreigner meets the local merchant. The foreigner finds a fascinating indigenous artifact and he purchases it from the merchant at three or four times its fair market price. The foreigner can hardly believe that he has paid so little for so exotic and so rare an item; he can hardly wait to show it to his friends and brag about his adventures in the Far East. The local merchant is already telling his friends how he has made a fat profit off of a naïve foreigner, triumphantly fanning himself with crisp bills. This is a comedy where the joke is equally on everyone, so no one is more the victim and no one less the victor; as long as we all play our parts as written, everyone is happy. I had no wish to undermine the evenhandedness of such a scene.

So, to satisfy the requirement of the script, I asked the merchant the price of the *belu* and I was quoted, as I had heard them rehearse earlier, "six dollars."

"I'll give you four dollars," I offered. I knew I could have purchased the marionette for two dollars, but to deprive him of his profit of a few additional dollars would be simply unconscionable. He was a poor merchant struggling to stay afloat while his country's economy, due to two decades of mismanagement by the military regime of Burma and half a decade of economic sanction by foreign countries, was sinking faster than a galleon in a tempestuous sea. He probably made in a month less than what an average American made in a day. Two dollars, though less than the cost of a sandwich in San Francisco, is enough to provide a large family with a huge chunk of beef or pork for dinner in Rangoon. And affordable meat, grieved many Burmese I had met, was increasingly becoming a rarity. Every Shylock deserves a few drops of mercy, and the Shylocks of Bogyoke Market, being the skinniest ones I had seen, certainly deserved a few pounds of flesh. I gave the stall owner four dollars and received in return a demon in a brown bag.

As I walked down the aisle, a sickly boy of twelve or thirteen approached me.

"Hey mister, hey mister," he addressed me, pulling my sleeve. "Where you from?" he asked, forging a smile out of his sunken cheeks with some effort.

"America," I answered.

"Burma," he cried, and then pounded once on his thin chest, inside which I could almost hear his little organs whiz and buzz like the internal mechanisms of an overworked motor. "America," he cried, and then patted me once on the arm. "Friends," he announced, rubbing his forefingers together to indicate that the two countries were allies. I was tempted to tell him that the state of current relations between the two countries resembled the friction between his fingers more than the closeness of the fingers. But there was no time for such in-depth political analysis—he was already beginning his pledge of allegiance to America.

"I like America," he declared, adopting temporarily the solemnity of someone taking the witness stand in a trial. "America number one." He raised his thumb up and jabbed the air with it once.

Having thus declared his devotion to America, the little burgeoning capitalist began offering me an array of businesses, in a series of gestures and sparsely worded sentences that sometimes seemed to echo the vocabulary of Mr. Kyaw Oo. (His presence in the market on a weekday afternoon being a good indication that he had chosen entrepreneurism over education, I would not be the least bit surprised if he had actually been receiving English lessons from Mr. Kyaw Oo free of charge.)

"Got money? Change money? I give you good price."

"No, but thanks."

"Want girls? Pretty girls, good price." That is to say, he could get me "really pretty *Barmees* girls, really cheap."

"No, thanks."

"Want postcards? Beautiful postcards? Look, look." Like a magician, he pulled a deck of cards out of nowhere. He unfolded the clear plastic sheet that linked and held them together, and they flew out of his tiny palms, flipping and flopping like frightened pigeons. Because he liked Americans, he would let me have the plastic sheet at no extra cost.

"No."

Now that he had exhausted all his enterprises, he dropped the air of professionalism and began begging. "Mister, mister," he cried, "please give me some money." I gave him the loose change—about twenty-five kyats—in my wallet. He thanked me, and he renewed his earlier devotion: "American, number one, the best."

Every day, squalid and underfed children in Burmese schools learn that they owe their good fortune to the wisdom and generosity of the Army. They are reminded, repeatedly, that the Army protects the country from enemies within and without, domestic and foreign. On national holidays, they are herded into a park to watch the parade. They are instructed to hang laurels on riffle barrels when foot soldiers in faded uniforms march by, and to smile and wave when generals in black Mercedes drive by. There is usually live television coverage of the day-long event, so those at home, should they choose to tune in to one of the two government-controlled channels (still the *only* two channels available in the country at the time I was there), are most likely to see soldiers marching in a circle for hours, like a bunch of clockwork toys or a company of amateur actors poorly reconstructing Caesar's triumphant return to Rome.

General Ne Win, who took control of the country in a coup in 1962, was a member of the legendary 30 comrades who, during the Second World War, fought heroically against the Japanese forces under the leadership of General Aung San. Ne Win believed, and wanted every Burmese to believe, that he was the savior of Burma; every history book published by the government press in Burma included a lengthy chapter of epic proportion on how he rescued the country from its post-independence political turmoil, the text invariably accompanied by a picture in which he and Aung San appeared together, to suggest the legitimacy of his authority in the absence of Aung San. The picture showed him lurking in the unfocused and shadowy background, like a specter, and Aung San looming in the foreground, like the large bronze statue that presently guards the entrance of Aung San Park.

From 1962 to 1988, for over a quarter of a century, Ne Wing ruled the country by decree, imprisoning, exiling, and executing those who opposed him and his regime. In his reign, the Army rapidly established its authority behind every sector of the government; like an oppressive dark-green scenery that overcasts the vivacity of a lighthearted comedy, it remains the incongruous backdrop of civil institutions to this day.

In 1988, shortly after suppressing a nationwide protest by ordering the Army to gun down unarmed protesters, killing an undisclosed number in a single afternoon, General Ne Win announced his retirement. By then, his Burmese Way to Socialism (which was neither ideologically Burmese nor theoretically Socialist) had succeeded where English Colonialism and Japanese Fascism had failed-it had led the country into a state of unprecedented destitution. But, many believed, he exercised considerable power even in his retirement, continuing to draw the strings that animated the present administration like a puppet master behind the curtain. He fell from favor and was branded a traitor only recently, in March 2002, when he became implicated in his kin's alleged conspiracy to overthrow the government.

The headmistress of the school I attended often reminisced during assemblies, recounting how she, in her youth, braved the batons of the English police officers to stage demonstrations or organize strikes against colonial authorities. But this patriotic woman, who had fiercely fought against oppression, ruled the little kingdom that was hers with tyrannical severity. She rejected, in a nationalistic spirit that approached xenophobia, everything foreign, from cigarettes to rock and roll, and she seemed to believe, with sincerity, that in doing so she was protecting her native culture from the invasion of foreign cultures.

"You young people are spoiled," she declared. "You are undisciplined, unrefined, and you do not know what it means to love your country or your people. When we were young, we made a point of only wearing clothes made domestically. But look at you young men these days, wearing T-shirts with horrible pictures, and those ugly pants." She was referring to the psychedelic image (the album cover of Yellow Submarine) printed on someone's shirt and a pair of bell bottoms on someone else.

Long hair on men, she ruled, was a foreign trend far more influential than rock and roll or bell bottoms and needed to be curtailed. "If I catch any of you young men with your hair below the collar," she raged, "I will personally cut it off." Everyday, she stood behind the main gate, poised with a pair of scissors in her hand. Should she see a teenage male with long hair walk through the gate, she would give him an instant trimming. On an occasion that I witnessed, the gray-haired headmistress unceremoniously charged at her victim and, grabbing him by his collar, proceeded to snip off a large quantity of his hair, the result of this impromptu styling session being a hairdo that was somewhere between a crew cut and a flattop.

Since I also wore my hair long, I risked being guillotined. I managed to evade her barbershop blades by escaping every day through a small door—a dog hole—behind the school canteen. But my timid Burmese teacher, a soft-spoken young woman who joined the teaching profession soon after she graduated from college, found the threat posed by my rebellious hairdo a bit too difficult to ignore.

"You know," she observed, "your hair is too long. If she sees you, she'll cut it off right away. And, since you are primarily in my charge, if that happens, I'm afraid I'll get reprimanded too. I don't like it."

"I know," I argued, "but I don't think long hair is a foreign trend—Burmese courtiers from ancient times wore long hair, coiled in circles and wrapped in silk scarves."

"But are you going to wear your hair in a bun the way they did?" she asked.

"Well," I answered, "no."

"Then," she decided, "I'll have to trim it before she sees it."

This, far too often, is how revolutionaries become tyrants, and how simpletons like my Burmese teacher, by accepting and enforcing the nonsensical rules imposed upon them without questioning, end up serving the tyrants.

Tyrants rarely see themselves for what they are; they are more likely to view themselves as national heroes. They are far more theatrical than they will ever admit. They are temperamental celebrities, each surrounded by an expensive entourage of body-guards and buffoons. Their political speeches are musical numbers that switch keys every so often and always fade away in the end. Their electoral processes are so meticulously choreographed that they know the final outcomes beforehand. And their ministers, like choruses, echo whatever economic or foreign policies the tyrants see fit to adopt; the ambitious ones might even venture to give the tyrants some bad advice once in a while as suggested by Mr. Kyaw Oo in his joke. But all of them, being too insensitive to *give the people what they want* (which is the first rule of good entertainment), invariably end up putting on bad shows. Nothing looks as silly on stage as fools who behave like sages. And nothing is as detrimental to the integrity of a drama as villains who insist on being heroes, or actors who refuse to leave the stage after the curtain has dropped.

There *are* demons in Burma. They are easy to spot because they wear, beside stiff green uniforms and conspicuous brass medals, elaborate headdresses with military insignias. They are not sold in the mar-ket, but they can be bought; they tend to be quite a bit overpriced. They are incarnations of *minthas*, *minthamis*, and *wungyis* who fare lavishly in their *nandaws* while virtuous men and women of Burma pimp, peddle, and panhandle to barely survive.

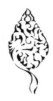

Mya Nan Nwe
of Botataung

By the bank of Rangoon River, where deserted jetties in different degrees of corrosion rise and fall with the languor of Burmese spinsters bathing and gossiping in a muddy creek at twilight, stands Botataung Pagoda—a gilded structure with a cylindrical base that tapers into an elegant pinnacle through countless swirling layers. A classic beauty in a surrounding of great industrial decay, exposed and defenseless, save the delicate parasol sheltering its head, the pagoda resembles an enchanting courtesan who accidentally finds herself among resentful crones.

What I remember mostly of the pagoda is its annual fair. Populated with vendors crouching beneath flickering street lamps, the residential blocks surrounding the pagoda became a fairground. Displayed on trays and laid out on pavements were quaint mementos, such as cardboard masks of smiling kings and chuckling demons, and paper dolls that flapped their arms and spread their legs when the strings behind them were pulled. Some of the more exotic local delicacies, such as skewered sparrows (grilled, with heads and wings still attached, past golden brown to a shiny charcoal-black) and deep-fried locusts (sold in large cones constructed of banana leaves held together by toothpicks), were enough to churn even the strongest stomachs.

The biggest attraction was the large movie screen enclosed within a series of removable bamboo partitions. At the gate of this make-shift amphitheater rose a 15-foot poster depicting various climactic scenes from *The Clash of the Titans*. The Olympian Zeus, rendered in acrylic by a local artist, looked more like a Burmese patriarch and less like Sir Laurence Olivier, who played the part. Inside, jumpy images from a hand-operated projector fought to remain steady on the screen. The agitation of the images and the breezes from Rangoon River added an atmospheric touch to the battles and tempests on screen.

From the loudspeaker, the projectionist provided the voice-over that was missing, complete with an immediate translation of the dialogues between the characters, each part vocally distinguished by an alternate pitch: *Here comes Mintha (Prince) Perseus to fight the sea monster and save Minthami (Princess) Andromeda chained to the rock . . . don't be afraid, I'm coming, I'll save you, he said . . . hurry, please, she yelled, she is trying to free herself but the chains are strong . . . and the sea monster is coming for her!* The translation was hardly accurate, but it captured the essence of what was happening on the screen, and it also served as a teaser for those who, unable to afford the admission fee, stood outside the bamboo walls and watched the movie on the partially visible edge of the screen.

"We should try to meet Mya Nan Nwe," announced my friend Aung Moe as we headed from the noisy fairground to the tranquil pavilions of the pagoda on our way home one night. At the time, we were two pubescent boys. We had just seen a bunch of Olympian titans, portrayed by Hollywood titans. We had chosen, unwisely, to seat ourselves at the forefront of the arena to optimize this divine cinematic experience. The result was a dull giddiness that would make us question our own sensory perceptions for weeks to come.

"Who?" I asked, partly because I couldn't hear very well, and partly because I didn't believe what I had just heard. "Botataung Mya Nan Nwe," he confirmed.

Botataung Pagoda, like the rest of the temples in Burma, is reputed to be haunted. Mya Nan Nwe, better known by her honorific name Botataung Mya Nan Nwe, is the beautiful maiden or the guardian spirit who, outfitted in regal costumes as ancient as her name, walks the pagoda's shadowy aisles in the absence of worshippers.

Sacred sites in Burma are believed to be guarded by minor deities known as *nats*. Due to its high volume of violent and unnatural deaths, Burma seems to have more *nats* than it knows what to do with. Since most *nats* are, according to the folklore and legends from which they emerge, victims of betrayal, intrigue, and murder in life, guardianship seems like the perfect afterlife vocation for them; having paid dearly for trusting too much too soon before, the spiritual remains of these individuals are likely to be more cautious and diligent than an average mortal.

Despite the great multitude of monasteries and temples in Burma, no post of guardianship seems to have been left vacant; in fact, after appointing one *nat* to each religious site (and more than one to some sites that are considerably larger than others), there are still a good number of *nats* left without appointment that they have to be distributed among secular sites. Hence the peculiar existence of house *nat* (*ain-saunk-nat*), road *nats* (*lan-saunk-nat*), village *nats* (*ywar-saunk-nat*), and fig tree *nats* (*nyaung-bin-saunk-nat*) in addition to monastery *nats* (*kyaung-saunk-nat*), and temple *nats* (*payar-saunk-nat*). Being of a lower order, the secular deities seldom receive the same reverence their religious counterparts enjoy; consequently, they offer their patrons protection that amounts to nothing. But the supply of spirits outweighs the demand of the *nat* profession by so much that the Burmese embrace without protest this illusion of codependency, which provides the surplus population of *nats* with respectable abodes and their patrons the pretense of protection.

On the street where I grew up, whenever someone was about to go on a lengthy journey, the journeyer's family sent for Mr. Lu Lay. Mr. Lu Lay had in his possession a sturdy wooden pole about five feet long and a doll house (a miniature version of a temple), inside which stood U Shin Gyi, the patron *nat* of journeyers, enshrined in the form of a brightly painted, loudly dressed clay figurine with a boyish expression. Upon the appointed evening, Mr. Lu Lay paid the family a visit; a scowling brown dwarf carrying a pole and a wooden box, he usually arrived at dusk to set up the equipment in front of his client's house.

The role of Mr. Lu Lay was a difficult one to define—neither a medium nor a priest, yet an essential party in invoking a deity, he fluttered between heaven and earth, eluding both the clergy and the laity. I often wondered how he was able to travel from his cottage on the edge of the city to his clients' houses in downtown; an arduous journey involving several transfers and several rides on overcrowded busses, it was a commute hardly fit for someone carrying a pole and a box. Yet, as if by divine providence, he always arrived on time. After mounting the portable shrine (by screwing the box's bottom onto the pole's top), he began summoning the *nat*, his incantations much obscured at times by his habitual chewing of betel-nuts.

"O U Shin Gyi, U Shin Gyi, Lord of Land and Lord of Sea, give us protection, grant us safety," he intoned, pausing to spit out the blood-red betel-juice in his mouth. "Preside over the journey of this good man, this devoted servant of yours, this . . . this . . . what's your name by the way?" He paused again, to ascertain the name of his client. "Preside over the journey of this good man, this devoted servant of yours, as he sails through the sea or rides through the land, and remove the obstacles in his path," he went on for a while before he paused and spat again. When he reached this point, the children in the neighborhood usually had him surrounded on all sides, their eyes carefully trained on the plate of sweet rice balanced on the edge of the shrine.

"Remove from his path the creatures of the underworld, the demons, the witches, the evil spirits, the . . . the . . . get away from there you little devil!" He screamed when he saw someone try to snatch the plate. "Conduct him through his journey, light his path, lead him through darkness, guard him from the unholy host, the beasts and the monsters . . . you foul imps, get away from there, I say!"

The process was again interrupted so that he could ward off the tiny fingers reaching for the plate. His incantations became indistinguishable from his outbursts beyond this point; he addressed the little minions from the neighborhood and the legions of hell in the same breath, often using the same pronouns interchangeably for both.

Thus he went on, pausing to spit and swear alternately. When he began reciting his final passage, which the children recognized as a cue that the ceremony was concluding, he held the pole tight in anticipation of the disorder that was about to follow. But the disorder invariably began before the ceremony could come to a proper end; leaping forward, the children began to grab the plate, and grains of rice flew everywhere.

The origin of the patron *nat* of journeyers, ironically, sounds like a cautionary tale against journeying. U Shin Gyi was reportedly a gifted musician; the terra cotta inside Mr. Lu Lay's shrine holds a harp close to its bosom. On the fateful voyage that eventually proved to be his last, U Shin Gyi passed the time plucking his instrument on the moonlit deck of the ship. Unfortunately for him, some sentimental mermaids swimming nearby overheard his rapturous music; the listeners were so enamored that they devised a plan to keep the musician forever for private performances. The obstacle to their union being the line that divided the immortals from the mortals, they decided to bring him to their plane of existence by making him immortal; they prepared to drown the ship with a tempest.

"We're going to drown!"

"What are we going to do?"

"We can sacrifice someone to appease the sea deities," suggested one person, presumably the captain who saw no hope in his own navigation skills.

"Who, who shall be thrown overboard?"

"We'll draw lots."

With the mermaids overseeing the process, it was not surprising that U Shin Gyi ended up drawing the short straw. So the young musician was tied to a heavy object (quite possibly his own musical instrument) and thrown overboard as a sacrifice to the sea. Notwithstanding the manner in which he had been re-routed from his intended destination, he subsequently became the patron *nat* of travelers in general, and sailors in particular.

Many Burmese men, finding few economic opportunities domestically, venture abroad to become sailors. And becoming a sailor on a foreign cargo ship is, in many ways, an expedition unto itself, often taking years of campaigning. It begins with the ambitious young man making repeated trips to numerous government offices, within which dwell institutional deities endowed with the power to bless or doom the young man's enterprise; fail to offer these gods fitting tributes and he shall never see the stern of a ship, for they are as unforgiving as the Olympian bunch headed by Zeus.

Having sailed through the bureaucratic sea, this young man must now take a plane to the foreign port where he is to begin his career as a sailor. And it is a respectable or even an enviable profession in Burma: "My son is a sailor on a Singaporean ship," one often hears a Burmese matriarch boast, as she offers tiny cubes of cheese neatly arranged on her good china; "we want a doctor or a sailor for our girl," specify parents of marriageable girls when they consult matchmakers. Because they earn in three or four years what an office clerk earns (legitimately) in his or her entire career, sailors are regarded as members of a higher social order. In the neighborhood where he lives, he is a celebrity; when he returns from a lucrative voyage, neighbors (and, sometimes, strangers) come to sample the chocolates he brings home, and to hear his epic tales.

But Burmese sailors do voluntarily what their patron *nat* did involuntarily: they often jump ship. During my trip to Rangoon, I met my former classmate's husband, who used to be a cadet aboard a cargo ship that regularly sailed from Taipei to Los Angeles. He remembered what he saw and felt when his ship approached the Los Angeles port.

"There was a huge *M*," he recollected, "sitting on top of a restaurant." Later, when he described the colors, it became irrefutably clear to me that the first thing he saw of America was a McDonald's—I supposed the ubiquitous yellow *M* was as much an emblem of America as the Statue of Liberty.

"The custom officer was a tall blond in a tight uniform," he said, "and she had really big . . . you know." He gestured, as if he was struggling to hold two huge cantaloupes close to his chest, to describe the anatomy of this custom officer. I told him that, being from Los Angeles, she could have easily had certain parts of her body *supersized* surgically, but the joke was lost on him.

"I seriously thought about leaving the ship," he confessed, "but I remembered my wife, and my daughter, and what my disappearance would do to them." He continued, lowering his voice and gazing at his wife, who was feeding his daughter on a sofa nearby. "I could have left, found a job there, and eventually, when I became an American citizen, return to Burma to bring my family over." I knew of many who did exactly what he was describing. "But you know how it is in Burma. People would say things about me; they would say that I had abandoned my wife and my daughter. I could write them and reassure them that I would be coming back for them someday, but it would be a long time before I could do that, and it could be quite unbearable for them. Who was going to look after them till then?"

"Sometimes I wondered what might have happened," he pondered, in a heady mixture of doubt and regret, like an aging Odysseus remembering the day he gave up Calypso. Seen through the windows of the cabin on his claustrophobic cargo ship, Los Angeles appeared before him like a higher plane of existence—the tall, blond inhabitants, with bellies and thighs that have been chiseled to perfection by repeated pushups and reconstructive surgeries, might well be immortals; and the Ferraris and Alfa Romeos were the winged stallions of the gods.

I can see why this Burmese Odysseus, strongly tied though he was to his Penelope by unimpeachable devotion, must have been tempted to leap overboard into the arms of those teenage sirens roller-skating near Santa Monica Beach; their giggles were songs that no deprived sailor from an impoverished country could possibly resist. His life back home and his time on board being of restriction and parsimony, after a decadent feast of quarter-pound burgers and crispy fries (with a visit to a strip club or a topless bar on the side), he probably felt the same kind of blissful amnesia that shipwrecked Ithacans experienced on the land of lotus-eaters. Under these conditions, being thrown overboard didn't sound too bad; it was being trapped on board that he feared.

A sailor who abandons ship has to endure a kind of temporary death. He hides in anonymity and illegality, evading immigration officers, while his wife and children, torn between hope and embarrassment, wonder if they will ever see him again; few are those who return to earth after entering paradise. But if he does reappear one day, transformed and unrecognizable in a new skin (of Silver Tab Levis trousers and T-shirts that bear fascinating names such as Yosemite or Magic Mountain), he is embraced in tearful joy and his emergence from oblivion is celebrated with feasts and festivities that last days or even weeks. But even fewer are those from paradise who return to live on earth permanently; the soil, though suitable for unrefined soles, proves too vile for sanctified feet and sooner or later the visitor returns to the City of Angles, literally flying off. Those who have been fortunate enough to hear his sermon on celestial comfort (of gigantic shopping malls and multiplex cinemas) are instantly converted: "Take me with you," they plead. They know that they must first endure a transitory death before they can enter paradise. But, more importantly, they now know that they too can be reborn, out of their miserable existence into a new one of shining glory. To them, the fate that befalls their patron *nat* is less a terrible doom and more a blessing; they pray for it fervently. So they leave, quite literally by the shiploads every day, and their motherland, drained of her youthful energy, prematurely succumbs to the slow death of an unattended invalid.

"I know of a *gata* that can summon a dead person's spirit," revealed Aung Moe, on the night he decided to meet the guardian spirit of the pagoda. *Gatas* are short prayers or chants which, when recited successfully, enable the chanter to perform certain supernatural deeds; summoning a restless spirit is but one of the many unholy miracles achievable by *gatas*. There is a *gata* for every imaginable exploit. The longer ones, which can take hours to recite in their entirety, are reserved for public ceremonies and religious rites. The shorter ones range from passages employed by those otherwise handicapped in amorous affairs to bewitch their potential mates, to apologetic phrases uttered to elicit pardon from certain deities; finding himself far from public toilets, a Burmese pedestrian may relieve himself underneath a secluded fig tree, but he does so only after he has, in a hastily composed (and hastily delivered) speech of atonement or a *gata*, expressed his regret to the tree's guardian *nat*.

"I had it memorized because I heard it read numerous times by the monks during an exorcism," he confessed, hardly suspecting that, despite my nonchalance, the source of his esoteric knowledge was making me queasy. "They were using it to force the spirit of the dead person to come out of hiding so they could properly order it to go away," he reasoned, "but I don't see why the same *gata* wouldn't work if I use it to invite the guardian spirit to come out." He was overcome with excitement as he spoke, as though he had just unearthed some lost volume of alchemy, a discipline he was no stranger to.

"If this is the *gata* to order a stubborn spirit around," I tried to dissuade him, "the pagoda guardian might be put off by the harsh wording of it. Maybe you should try to learn the right *gata* first."

It soon became apparent to me that my mystic friend was quite willing to incur the guardian's wrath if, by doing so, he could provoke her into appearing briefly. If someone else other than Aung Moe *was* attempting to perform this rite, similarly using a *gata* that might or might not be entirely appropriate, there would have hardly been any cause for concern, and I would rather watch in amusement than intervene. But Aung Moe was the one performing the rite, so I didn't want to take a chance. He was not one to be underestimated; however absurd his endeavor was, there was always a possibility that he just might succeed. Only one month after he had first confessed to me he had been reading books on how to play the violin, he invited me up to his attic, above his grandmother's house, and fiddled the theme from *Dr. Zhivago* on a used violin he had recently acquired, from a heartbroken musician who had decided to become a monk. His performance, despite his lack of tenure, was almost perfect, save a few flat notes that could have easily been caused by a bad string. He had also surprised me by reading my palm soon after he began studying palmistry. I could hardly remember how accurate his predictions were, but he pronounced his findings with such authority and conviction that I couldn't help but feel some trepidation.

"This will do," he proclaimed, dropping to his knees on a quilt mat before an altar. A suitable site for his experiment thus picked, he began breathing intensely in preparation for his meditation. Knowing all hope of communication would be lost once he entered his meditative trance, I desperately appealed to his remaining faculties.

"Listen," I addressed him, "maybe you shouldn't do this. This could be dangerous—there's no saying what she might do when she appears."

"Don't you want to meet an immortal?" he asked me enticingly.

Mya Nan Nwe was renowned for her mesmerizing beauty. I envisioned the loose-robed, ample-bosomed immortals I had just seen in *The Clash of the Titans* just half an hour earlier—Aphrodite and Hera played by Ursula Andress and Claire Bloom. I recalled the climatic scene, during which Princess Andromeda (who, according to the projectionist, was also an immortal) struggled to free herself from iron cuffs and chains; her skirt was torn along the seam so that her thighs came into view every time she moved, and she moved frequently. Perhaps I should stay, I thought.

"So is it true," I asked, "that Mya Nan Nwe is incredibly beautiful?"

"Yes, it's been said that she is irresistible. As a matter of fact, some of those who meet her never quite recover from the shock."

"What do you mean?"

"Well, I knew a man who accidentally saw her once. He was not supposed to see her, but he ended up in the pagoda late one night, and, anyhow, to make a long story short, he saw her briefly."

It was inconceivable to me that someone could *accidentally* meet an immortal. Only experiments like the one he was conducting now, I thought, could accomplish this. Then, I recalled the heart-broken musician from whom he had inherited his first violin.

"Poor man," he continued. "He was never the same afterwards; when he spoke he didn't make a whole lot of sense, and he was always loitering near pagodas, whistling and singing unrecognizable songs, and he hardly ate or slept."

"You mean he became insane?"

"Sort of."

"Sort of? What do you mean?"

"I suppose it makes sense—being so beautiful and all, she must have made quite an impression on an ordinary man like him, so when she disappeared, not knowing what to do or where to go to find her, he became insane. He said she smiled at him before disappearing. That probably didn't help."

Before I could utter another word, he cupped his hands together and made a pledge to the cross-legged Buddha inside the altar. It was impossible to hear the whole pledge since he had solemnly dropped his voice to an inaudible pitch. But I was able to piece together fragments and phrases and came to a fairly good understanding of what his pledge was—in essence, he vowed that he would recite this particular *gata* (which he referred to by a lengthy name in *Pali*, an ancient language hardly spoken outside Buddhist monasteries) "nine hundred and ninety-nine times," and if he was able to carry out his promise, he wished to be rewarded with the sight of Mya Nan Nwe.

In Burmese numerology, *nine* is a number to be reckoned with. But so highly elusive is the logic employed by Burmese numerologists to determine the exact manner in which it is to be treated, they cannot seem to agree on a specific formula. On one occasion, a client may be advised to "offer nine different types of flowers to nine different *nats* chosen at random" in order to ensure success, and on another, the same client may be warned, quite possibly by the same pavement palmist or curbside astrologer, to avoid *nine* at all cost: "Don't take Number Nine bus, or any bus with a license plate that ends in nine." If the client protests that, due to limited commuting routes available to him, he is unable to comply with this demand, then the numerologist may suggest a counter-measure: "Then be sure to reflect on *Gone Daw Ko Par* (The Nine Principal Virtues of Buddha) whenever you board the bus."

The urban legend (purported to be based on a truthful account) of nine pilgrims who went to Kyaik Htiyo Pagoda suggests that any pilgrimage undertaken by a party of nine is doomed to fail; but, as the story proves, there are ingenious solutions for stubborn pilgrims who are unwilling to compromise. Discouraged by bad omens, bad dreams, and successive accidents, the nine pilgrims went to a monastery and asked the abbot to bless their pilgrimage before proceeding.

"How many of you are there?" asked the abbot.

"Nine," they answered.

"That's the problem," diagnosed the abbot.

Then he prescribed a numerological fix: "Take this," he said, handing them a piece of rock, "and treat it as if it were an additional member of your traveling party throughout the rest of your journey." In some versions of the story, the pilgrims merely carried the stone inside their luggage. In others, they went as far as giving it a seat of its own during meal times, completing the process by ordering an additional dish (of fried rice, fried noodles, or whatever was deemed suitable for a rock's consumption) for their solid, ethereal companion. Thus, with the imaginary tenth pilgrim by their side, the nine original pilgrims were able to deceive the malicious forces at work and complete the journey without any more mishaps.

With the auspicious *nine* weighing heavily on my mind, I began assessing the situation I was in. Even by a conservative estimate, it would take a full night to recite 999 times a *gata* of any given length. Were my friend successful in his attempt, the guardian spirit of the pagoda would appear briefly, but this temporal bliss was accompanied by the risk of permanent insanity. No matter what the outcome was, no good could come of it. And I sincerely believed that he had a good chance to succeed. This worried me; I didn't mind giving up a good night's sleep for the chance to meet an immortal spirit, but the thought of losing my mind terrified me. So, while my friend was reciting his *gata* for the tenth or the eleventh time, I quietly fled.

When I went out for breakfast the next morning, I sighted him; looking feral and disheveled, he was slurping noodles in a stall several blocks away from the pagoda. I approached him timidly, convinced that he had actually succeeded in the experiment the previous night and, as a result, had gone crazy. When he saw me, he raised his chin, which emerged from the bowl of broth, drenched with malodorous dark liquid, like a primeval beast rising from the depth of the ocean.

"So did you see her?"

"No."

"What happened?"

"I think I messed up," he answered. "Around midnight, I became extremely sleepy and tired, so it was quite possible that I skipped quite a few lines from the gata—or, maybe I said the right words but in the wrong order. After that, I knew there was no longer any hope, so I went back to the fairground and watched *The Clash of the Titans* again."

He shrugged, belched, and dived right back into his bowl of broth.

On the last morning of my recent trip to Rangoon, six hours before my flight back to San Francisco, I went to bid Min Min, one of my former classmates, farewell. She asked if I would like to do anything else in Rangoon before my departure. I reflected on how, a decade ago, I had left Aung Moe behind in a pavilion in Botataung Pagoda while he was invoking the spirit of Mya Nan Nwe. The pagoda was within walking distance from Min Min's house.

"I want to see Mya Nan Nwe," I announced.

"You know what they say about Mya Nan Nwe, don't you?" she asked, with a look of gentle caution.

"That she is so beautiful that I might become insane if I meet her?"

"I'm just worried that you might not want to leave if you meet her."

"I don't think you need to worry about that," I said, laughing. "My father is coming to pick me up to go to the airport, so he'll make sure that I leave."

"Then, come on, let's go visit Mya Nan Nwe."

I thought she was simply playing along, but I realized she actually intended to take me somewhere when she put her sandals on and walked out, signaling me to follow.

"Where are we going?"

"To Botataung Pagoda, of course."

Somewhere within Botataung Pagoda, there is a labyrinth with mosaic walls; its interior is similar to the inside of a kaleidoscopic tube. Through a towering gilded gate one enters this labyrinth. To arrive at the center of this labyrinth, one follows either the footsteps of the worshippers ahead or one's own instinct, whichever one trusts more. But this is a Buddhist labyrinth; its simple and elegant geometric design serves not to misguide but to lead the wayfarer towards the center. It is impossible to get lost in this labyrinth; so long as one walks forward, one inevitably ends up at the center, where one meets not the Minotaur, but one's own destiny.

Attached to a rotating pillar at the center, a multi-level prayer-wheel spins squeakily, alternately bringing silver bowls with different labels, such as "good health" or "success in romance" or "victory," closer to one and then farther away. But, of course, wishes don't come free; one has to toss coins and folded bills into the desired bowl to win the appropriate wish. It is difficult but, with good aim, good luck, and good practice (perhaps on the 99th attempt), one just might manage to land a crisp $1 bill into the bowl that guarantees "nirvana." (One German tourist, I witnessed on my last visit, overcame this impossible feat by folding his bill into a wide-winged paper-plane prior to tossing it.) But because the bowl of "nirvana" is on too high a level, with too many obstructions between it and the rest, most of the bills land instead in the realm of earthly pleasures, such as "car," "lottery," or "money."

When I was growing up in Rangoon, during late afternoon hours my parents used to listen to Buddhist sermons recorded on cassette tapes. The cool cement floor directly beneath the ceiling fan being the only refuge from the intolerable tropical heat, we all sat cross-legged, each holding a cup of tea and a fritter, around a battery-operated Sony cassette player and listened to parables from Buddhist Cannons retold by old monks, some of whom were renowned for their unmatched portrayal of certain tragic roles: "Get the three-tape epic about the notorious murderer *Inguli Mala* by the Venerable Kya Ni Kan," recommended our neighbor. "The final scene is guaranteed to make you cry."

Traditionally, the moment when a villain finally gains enlightenment is the meatiest portion of the whole parable, for it is here that the villain is given a chance to express his or her regret, grief, and repentance in a lengthy soliloquy. It is quite common for some of the sensitive listeners, moved by the remorseful aria of the villain, to break down when the parable reaches its operatic finale; most of these tapes being live-recordings of sermons given in large auditoriums (released afterwards with little or no effort to edit or reduce the background noises), one can hear, between occasional coughs and sneezes, a few listeners sniffle and blow their noses as they refrain from weeping openly.

I recall that in one of the tapes, the narrator, an aging monk with an unsteady baritone, described the episode in which Gautama Buddha proved the notion of self to be an illusion. Imagine the scene within a monastery located somewhere in the City of Vesali in 500 B.C. India, with Gautama on a podium and row after row of his shaved-headed, saffron-robed disciples below him; whenever they prostrated in response to a remark he made, the simultaneous motion of this human sea flowed like powerful tidal waves.

"*Chit tha* (beloved son)," Gautama addressed someone who had been vehemently challenging the scripture. "You keep saying *I, I, I*—show me where this *I* is."

"Why, here *I* am," responded the challenger, patting himself on the chest. The whole assembly came to a complete silence.

"But that's your chest, isn't it?" asked Gautama.

"I mean this is *me*," answered the challenger, waving his arms.

"Those are your arms you are waving," corrected Gautama.

"But these are *my* arms," said the challenger, "and these are *my* legs, and these *my* eyes, and this *my* nose. They are what *I* am."

"Should they become separated from your body," asked Gautama, "should your arms and legs be hewed off, your eyes gouged out, and your nose detached, would you then still claim that they are who you are?"

The person examined every one of his limbs in question and, being someone of stark imagination, proceeded to envision them torn off from his body and thrown across the floor like pieces of beef or poultry displayed on a butcher's table.

"Of course not," he answered, "then they would just be arms, legs, a pair of eyes, and a bloody nose."

"Then I asked you again," repeated Gautama calmly, "where is this *I* that you speak of?"

"My mind," answered the challenger, employing in desperation an early variation of Descartes' famous I-think-therefore-I-am argument centuries before the philosopher's birth. " I can think, I can reason, I can talk, and I can feel, therefore my mind is what *I* am."

"Where does your mind reside? What do you think with?" asked Gautama.

"My head, my brain, of course," responded the frustrated challenger.

"Then when your head is removed from your body . . ." This was still more or less a primitive age, and decapitation was the monarchy's favorite way of dealing with rebellious peasants; it was not difficult to imagine what it would be like to have one's head chopped off.

"All right, all right," interrupted the challenger, "I get it—then it would just be a stinking rotten head, but it wouldn't be who *I* am."

"Then I asked you again," repeated Gautama emphatically, "where is this *I* that you speak of?"

Walking through the labyrinth of Botataung Pagoda with Min Min, looking into the tiny mirrors buried inside its walls, I saw my own image—my *self*—shattered into countless unrecognizable pieces: here were my eyes, the left one separated from the right one; here was an arm that belonged either to me or to the person standing next to me; and here was my necktie, twisted, and deformed. Suddenly, awakened thus by fragmented reflections, everything became clear—no longer significant was the notion that I was a foreigner, or that I was a native, or that I was a native who had forsaken my motherland to become a foreigner, or that I was a Burmese, or that I was a Chinese, or that I was an American. They had all along been nothing but components of my self. And, right before my eyes, my self had been dissected into tiny particles of light reflected on the mosaic walls around me. The self, according to the old monk who had so convincingly imitated Gautama, was not real; it was merely an illusion. Even my dismembered body parts visible on the walls were not real; they too were merely reflections and therefore illusions. Here, finally, all the seemingly irreconcilable colors and patterns inside a kaleidoscope merged and became one, or dissolved and became nothing. And here the elaborate design of a mandala that had taken years to construct suddenly turned to sand and dust. Here was the resolution to, and the dissolution of, my foreigner/native identity crisis.

"We thought you got married and moved far away," said Min Min, referring to the three years— my transitory death—following my immigration to America. "You didn't write, you didn't call, and you didn't even send a postcard. Whenever we got together, we talked about you, and, a few of us even suggested—as a joke of course—that you might be dead."

"I knew you might think that," I said, "and that's why I came back." The first night I arrived in Rangoon, I had gone to her house, unannounced, and surprised her. After opening the door, and after a delay of several seconds, she asked, "Is it really you, or are you a ghost?"

I *was* a ghost. A decade ago, severing all my ties with Burma, I moved to a different realm without so much as a backward glance, so Min Min and the rest of my friends, after some persistence, naturally gave up on me and buried me. Now, like a restless spirit returning to complete an unfinished task, I returned remorsefully to the city that was once mine. And, like an apparition that was a shadow of its former self, I wandered through deserted streets and temples at strange hours in a shape that was an eerie reminder of what I once was. But being a ghost myself, I reasoned, I had nothing to fear from another ghost—Mya Nan Nwe.

"There she is," announced Min Min as we stepped into the shade of a pavilion. Once within, the bright afternoon light dissolved. We transitioned from light to darkness so swiftly that my vision became a blur. But I saw her, the mythical guardian of the temple, once I regained my sight—a life-size clay-figure decked out in full court regalia, she knelt serenely before a series of flowerpots and shrines. She seemed weighed down by her gold-plated headdress and her shawls, layer after layer of them on her shoulders and around her neck, all donated by faithful servants and worshippers, each of whom, undoubtedly, prayed for a boon in return for his or her offering.

A Burmese deity is rarely at peace—worshippers constantly pester it with petitions of all kinds. If the deity, motivated by kindness, begins to fulfill the wishes of a few benefactors, they return for more; the more boons it bestows, the more petitions it receives. As its efficiency becomes renowned through word of mouth, the collection boxes before its shrine overflow with large bills. But, at this point, the number of petitions from the steady stream of worshippers has increased to such an extent that the deity can no longer hear them all; like the incoming mail on an overworked clerk's desk, the majority of the prayers are left unanswered. Eventually the worshippers lose faith in the deity and they cease to come. Only then, having fallen from favor, is the deity finally left to its peaceful solitude in its forgotten temple. But even this, as proven by the Buddhist Law of Impermanence, is temporal; after a while, threatened by the prospect of obsolescence, the deity begins granting boons again. Thus, perpetual and cyclical, a Burmese deity lives between fame and disgrace alternately.

"Aren't you going to wish for anything?" asked Min Min.

"No," I replied.

"What? Too American to pray to a Burmese goddess?" scoffed my friend.

While my friend was saying her prayers to Mya Nan Nwe, I took my camera out. When I was able to see both my friend and Mya Nan Nwe in the same frame, I pressed the button. I didn't remember if I had had my flash on or off. I had but lifted my forefinger from the button when I heard the film within the chamber automatically rewind. It was my last roll of film and I was leaving Burma in a few hours. So this, I realized, was to be the last impression of Burma I captured. A week later, when the pictures were developed, I was to discover that, despite vivid colors on Min Min's image in the same frame, Mya Nan Nwe's image did not register; as elusive as she had always been, she appeared as numerous shadowy outlines. My sister blamed the poor quality of the picture to my unsteady hand whereas I attributed it to the immateriality of spirits. "So you've seen what you came to see," reminded my friend. "Now it's time to go."

From within the shelter of the pavilion, I looked out into the field. Hot dust rose from the ground like clouds in a sandstorm. An army of flower sellers, reinforced by a horde of young beggars, guarded the gate; they wrestled with one another, each struggling to be the first to offer me an overpriced bouquet or to demand a boon. Old green trucks, which had apparently outlived the English officers who brought them to Burma during World War II, toddled along ill-defined roads, halting, coughing, and screeching with senile uncertainty at every turn.

Brutal reality undermines everything quaint in Burma; few outsiders are capable of enduring what most Burmese suffer with dignity and humility every day. Yet, like a desert traveler mesmerized by a mirage, I found myself drawn to the deceptive charm of Burmese life. It was time for me to leave, but I was reluctant to go. Travelers are a strange and stubborn bunch; contrary to the dictates of rationality, they seek ease in discomfort, reward in depravity, meaning in absurdity, and a surprising number of them report that they actually find what they seek.

Amidst chaos and cacophony—the screaming of flower sellers, the pleading of beggars, and the rattling of vehicles that were carefully welded back together long after they had passed their intended lifespan—I heard the silvery music of wind chimes from the pinnacle of the pagoda, their rhythm as regular as the cycle of death and rebirth, their cadence as reassuring as the celestial promise of peace and freedom.

"Too late," I joked. "I've seen Mya Nan Nwe, and I don't want to leave." But I was more earnest than I had realized at the time.

The Ghost

The ghost of a deceased Burmese is believed to briefly return to his or her former dwelling place exactly a week after the burial. But the ghost, being of Burmese origin in particular, might abuse his visitation right and refuse to leave altogether, for a Burmese is extremely fond of his or her family and friends and wants to spend as much time as possible with them—even in afterlife. But the survivors and the loved ones (often but not always) understand better than the deceased that the living and the dead cannot coexist; therefore they usually make provisions to ensure that the visitor, though welcome, is discouraged from lingering, and the visitation, while rejoiced by all, is kept strictly a brief reunion.

But such an occasion inevitably involves sentimental farewells and conciliatory remissions that can go on and on if left unsupervised. So the presence of a levelheaded third party is certainly preferable. A team of Buddhist monks is best suited for this task, for they are required to renounce not only their worldly possessions but also their human passions when they were ordained. As for their number, seven or eight might be adequate, but nine, which has some added benefits due to its numerological correlation to Buddha's Nine Principal Virtues, is definitely better. Minimalism is hardly a Burmese characteristic when it comes to religious ceremonies, but if economic hardship forces one to select instead a smaller, humbler team of monks for such an occasion, *three* is often recommended, for it signifies the Three Gems of Buddhism—*Paya* (The Enlightened One), *Taya* (The Dogma), and *Thanga* (The Monastic Order).

But, usually, no Burmese ritual—large or small, solemn or gay—can come to a proper conclusion unless every guest has been fed to his or her heart's content (and beyond his or her gut's capacity), and the excess food divided and dispatched to those who have been unable to come: "Eat as much as you can, and then take some home for your parents who couldn't come," a hostess might be heard urging a guest on such an occasion, as she sits on the floor and fans him from behind to keep him from drowning in a puddle of his own sweat, and the guest, who is laboring against his will to finish the third bowl of spicy fish-broth in order to avoid offending the hostess, can do little else but nod. It must also be noted that the excess food is hardly the result of an inexperienced hostess's poor estimate; it is generally the intention of the hostess to prepare food in quantity far exceeding what is required to satisfy the anticipated number of guests, because she knows that the neighbors who have opted to stay home still expect some leftovers, neatly parceled in banana leaves, to be delivered to them via an errand boy or another guest who happens to be passing through. Generosity is such an integral part of Burmese culture that the Burmese are likely to practice extravagant hospitality even in times of extreme deficiency.

So, when the seventh day arrives, the monks file into the former home of the deceased and, seated on a raised platform of some kind near the main entrance, begin reciting in *Pali* (a dead language only a scholarly ghost can comprehend) lengthy passages of sacred text, the summary of which might very well be, "Welcome back, farewell, please move on." If the spirit of the departed, bypassing the monks' reception, somehow manages to advance farther into his or her former home, then the heart-wrenching cries of the loved ones (whose lamentations are usually in vernacular and easier to understand than the monk's *Pali*) ought to serve as reminder that he or she must soon proceed to a different plane of existence.

I had for a long time struggled to understand who I was supposed to be. Like warring ethnic tribes of Burma, my national, cultural, and ancestral identities fought with one another. A lasting peace among them seemed finally possible when my notion of self, or selves, was eradicated within the labyrinth of Botataung Pagoda. But even after I had seen myself deformed, disfigured, and smashed into pieces, I found that I couldn't drop the notion of self altogether; I am extremely self-centered and I cannot dismiss the notion of self entirely. I have become too accustomed to the shifting colors of my kaleidoscope and the swirling patterns of my mandala; even if they turn my stomach and make me dizzy, I must retain them. These self-made ideas of myself are all I have to define who I am. Without them, I shall truly be lost. Given a choice, I choose to be misguided and found rather than enlightened and lost. So, leaving the wisdom exactly where I found it, I salvaged the remains of my shattered selves and came out of the labyrinth as unenlightened as I went in. Perhaps this is the only form of enlightenment possible for an irreligious man like me—that I am a ghost, a scavenger, forever doomed to grow and harvest immaterial, insubstantial shadowy illusions of self.

I disappeared, and a decade later, I resurfaced in Burma, choked with nostalgia like a ghost fumbling for a way home. I explored Rangoon like some timid traveler, full of expectation and apprehension. I renewed some old friendships. The familiar now looked exotic and the ordinary appeared foreign. If the ghost of someone departed a week ago is not allowed to prolong his or her final visit, then the ghost of someone who has been gone for nearly a decade certainly has no right whatsoever to insist that he or she be permitted to return home permanently. Whenever I exclaimed, "I wish I could stay forever in Burma," someone else always replied, "You can't." My old playmates and classmates knew, perhaps better than I did, that I did not belong in Burma anymore. Perhaps the power outage, the shortcut through the back of a morgue, and the dog hole on my first morning in Rangoon, after all, were Burma's way of discouraging me from lingering. A wish is a desire for an improbability, a request for a boon. Certain boons should never be granted, because granting ruins them. Longing is undeniably a misery, but disappointment is an even greater misery. In such cases, the divinities ought to ignore the pleas of the worshipper who knows no better.

When I was attending Rangoon University in the late 1980s, I heard rumors that the library was haunted by the specters of students massacred during an uprising in the late 1970s. People still talked about how, to subdue a number of protesters demanding political reform, the Army drove tanks and armored carriers into the campus and fired into the crowd. What gave this rumor credibility was another rumor, widely circulated among older students, that the library was constructed on top of a mass grave where the wounded students, some dead and others dying, were quietly and swiftly buried. The fact that this new library was erected soon after the bloody event, with efficiency and expediency uncharacteristic of government construction projects, also added weight to both of these rumors. In a country where newspapers lie and statesmen do their best to hide the truth, rumor is often the most reliable source of information.

At least one undergraduate student, according to yet another unsubstantiated rumor, had the misfortune of meeting some of the souls wandering lost, trapped inside the library. It was late in the evening and the library was about to close, but this particular student, who was still searching for a manuscript that would provide the quotation she needed to complete her paper, remained preoccupied among the tall, dusty shelves. And she heard what sounded like the whimpering of a pup coming from a dark corner. The source of the sound, she soon discovered, was a man, looking fatigued, leaning on a stool. The faint yellow light of a flickering 30-Watt bulb dangling from the ceiling made the man's shadow lurch back and forth on the wall. She noticed that he was drenched.

"You are sweating," she remarked. "Are you all right?"

"I'm fine," he responded, in a pitiable whelp, "but I'm horribly thirsty."

"I'll get you some water," she offered. "Just wait here."

When she returned with a cup of cool water from an earthen jar nearby, he immediately began drinking, holding the misshapen steel mug with trembling hands and pouring the content directly into his mouth. The veins on his neck slithered like worms and the cartilage in his throat climbed up and down like a frightened rat. When he was finished, she noticed that he began sweating profusely again, particularly in his abdomen.

"Please," he pleaded, "get me some more."

When she returned, he snatched the mug of water from her hand, mumbling incoherent apologies for his incivility, and drank as though it was his first cup of liquid in years. The process was repeated numerous times but the man's thirst seemed unquenchable by any amount of water, and he continued to perspire below the waist.

"Mister," asked the undergraduate at one point, "you have drank all the water. The jar is now empty. What is the matter with you?"

"I have a hole," he replied, water still dripping from his mouth. "I cannot hold water."

"What do you mean?" she asked, perplexed.

He lifted his shirt to reveal his stomach, and she saw in it a large hole—through it, she could read the names on the spines of books lined up on the shelves behind him.

"They shot us with tank cannons," he reminded her. "Don't you remember?"

The girl, seized by fear, ran down several flights of stairs and ended up in the lobby, panting, shuddering, and yelping. And she saw a solitary librarian, sweeping the floor.

"There is someone with a hole in his body," screamed the girl.

"What?" asked the librarian.

"I just met him upstairs," she explained. "He's got a huge hole in his stomach. Said he was shot by a cannon, it's horrible!"

"Oh," replied the librarian calmly, as he unbuttoned his shirt to reveal his abdomen to the girl. "You mean, something like this?" he asked, turning around to reveal a hole with gunpowder stains in his stomach.

At this point, according to the story, the unfortunate undergraduate fainted from shock.

In reality, however, the Burmese are not very likely to show someone, least of all an outsider, their wounds. Instead, they might do their best to hide their sufferings because, in their definition of hospitality, the host or the hostess is required to do his or her best to avoid oppressing the guest with concerns that are solely of his or her own. Burmese temples mesmerize foreigners with their gilded facades. The relief on their walls and woodcarvings often show smiling divinities granting boons to kneeling worshippers. Even the fanged demons standing beside the entrances of pagodas seem genuinely pleased to see the visitors. This is the image of Burma the ruling regime is selling to the world at large, and ironically, this is also the only image of Burma the ordinary Burmese are proud to share with the world.

In the literal sense, however, the Burmese do air their dirty laundry out in the open; on a sunny day in downtown Rangoon, walking through a street lined with multi-story apartment buildings, one is amazed at the wide variety of dingy, soggy undergarments (white T shirts with soiled armpits, checkered boxer-shorts, nylon brassieres, and so on) fluttering unabashed on wires extending out of the balconies.

But this is an indiscretion brought on by necessity, for the majority of them, finding laundry machines too costly, rely primarily on natural sunlight to dry their garments. They dry their tears, on the other hand, with much greater discretion. They almost never expose their personal tragedies to the general population the way the Americans do with ease and bravado on public airwaves. If, compelled by repeated requests, a Burmese is forced to disclose his or her sad life, the disclosure is very likely to be one tampered with reluctance, restraint, and embarrassment.

Many Burmese see their sons shot to death and their daughters raped under the military regime. And many more are rotting in unmarked prison cells for doing no more than marching along during an antigovernment demonstration or attending a pro-democracy conference. In remote regions, both government troops and rebel troops harass the impoverished inhabitants of the villages, and both sides take turns using them as porters and human shields, forcing them to walk across minefields carrying launchers and rifles. In spite of it all, the Burmese stubbornly refuse to bewail the injustice they suffer or the misery they are subjected to on a regularly basis. They are too proud, and consequently too embarrassed, to whimper and whine about their woeful existence like underdogs elsewhere. Instead, they bear it all with dignity, swallowing insults the way they eat bitter tea leaves.

But to someone who is fully aware of their plight, their mulish silence doesn't bring peace; instead, it amplifies their suffering. It is hard to accept the hospitality of a smiling Burmese matriarch who offers to put one up in the attic where her son used to sleep when one knows her son is serving time in jail for attending a political rally. Standing before Botataung Pagoda's gate, I gradually came to the sad realization that I no longer had the endurance necessary to survive in Burma. I could no longer bite my tongue and look the other way when faced with institutional insolence. And I could no longer listen to the timid pleas of countless famished children living in the shadows of temples, for I no longer possessed the religious stoicism of a Burmese. I was having difficulty coping with the temperature in December; if I had remained there, once April, the cruelest month of the year, arrived, I would have shriveled up like a pickled prune and died. In the past, I might have known how to live in Burma. But Burma now terrified me.

Burma haunted me because it too, in a way, was a ghost, unsuccessfully searching for a way back to a mythical time. The old timers, who considered themselves blessed because they had had a chance to live in better conditions, invariably began their ruminations with, "When we were young," and finished glumly with, "You kids were born too late," or, "You missed the good times." In between, they talked of the days when honest living was, though not the path to prosperity, still a possible means of survival. A free and cheerful people living under an oppressive totalitarian regime for nearly four decades has good reason to long for a way back to a different era—a time when one can read, write, speak, and think without fear.

Everywhere in Burma, there are decaying structures. They hint of a time when post-colonial Rangoon, bathed in a sort of afterglow, was still frequented by foreign dignitaries from all over; but they now stand, like haunted Victorian or Edwardian mansions, overdue for renovation and unfit for habitation (but shirts and shorts on sagging clothes lines prove hundreds of poor souls have no choice but to live in them). The Burma that the old timers knew was summarily court-martialed and shot after the military coup four decades ago. Deprived of the pomp and pageantry of a military funeral, it was laid to rest in an unmarked grave in a cemetery unknown to the outside world. The whole sad affair was executed with such a lack of due process that some parts of the world are just learning about the passing of dear old Burma for the first time. But evidently, on the seventh day after the burial, no one bothered to say a prayer for the returning ghost. So it lingers in everyone's mind and, being of Burmese origin, it flatly refuses to leave its loved ones.

But my motherland needs to move on. If she fails to realize or refuses to acknowledge this, someone ought to tell her that she is dead. No one should have to live with a specter. The sidecar master who makes his living paddling his wheels under the merciless sun for hundreds of miles without a hat, the baked-bean-seller who earns her meals walking from street to street with a loaded basket on her head, and the underage flower-seller who sells gardenias to cab drivers at the traffic light—they all deserve to live among the living, not among the dead.

Some may insist that the sidecar master, the bean-seller, and the flower-seller are all part of the romantic Burmese landscape that ought to remain unchanged. But preservation does not come cheap; preservation of a ghost is costly. And preservationists are rarely the ones who pay the bill. It is the sidecar master, the bean-seller, and the flower-seller of Burma that get squeezed, dried, salted, gutted, and dehydrated in the process of mummification; they are the ones that pay the price of preservation with their blood and sweat. Someone ought to mourn Burma's death, so that she knows she is now free to move on, to transmigrate to another realm. If no one is willing to undertake the somber task, then, however inappropriate it may be, the ghost of a former native must perform the ritualistic exorcism.

When the ghost of a native met the ghost of his motherland, they both realized their reunion could not last long. Each found it impossible to articulate his or her emotions to the other under the terrible constraint of time.

"You haven't changed a bit," observed mother Burma.

"But I have," protested her native son.

"You look pale," she said.

"You look pale," he said.

"Son," remarked the mother, "you've become too tall and too big—must be the milkshakes and hamburgers your stepfather has been feeding you. You cannot sleep in that little bed of yours in my attic anymore, and I don't think you still remember how to sleep on the cement floor either. Oh, I just don't know where to have you spend the night."

"I know mom," said the young man. "I'll be going home soon, so you don't need to worry." When she heard him refer to another place as "home," she felt a lump rising in her throat. "But I've got something important to say to you before I go," he ventured.

"What?" she asked.

"Mom," he broke the news reluctantly, "you're dead."

"What do you mean?" she asked, looking alarmed.

"You died a long time ago, mom," said the young man. "You're a ghost."

"I don't believe you," she replied furiously.

"Please," he begged, "believe me, for once."

"This is preposterous," she responded, sullenly.

"Mom," he urged, "you need to move on."

"Move on? To where?" retorted the old woman.

"Just go," he replied, "go where you have to go."

"I don't know where to go," she said, looking frightened.

"But you *must* go," he insisted.

"I want to take a look at the Strand Hotel one last time," she said, "and maybe ride the elevator too."

"Sure," agreed the young man, "but don't take too long."

"And, and," the old woman continued, "I want some apples from the Chin Hill too."

"Sure," he said, "whatever you like."

"But what about Shwe Dagon? I can't leave without visiting Shwe Dagon? And Botataung too, since it's on the way. Do I have time to stop at Bogyoke Market? And, and . . . ." She went on and on.

We meet, we part.

We live, we die.

We are reborn.

But we can never remain the same.

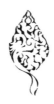

Afterword

On Christmas Eve, 2002, when our family's dinner conversation turned to current events in Burma, someone once again introduced the notion that Ne Win, Burma's former strongman, was dead. If true, this was blessed news indeed, but we knew better. Ever since his retirement from politics in 1988, and even before then, the boogeyman of Burma had periodically been reported to be dying, dead, or (my favorite) assassinated. Many of those reports, I suspect, were fueled by the Burmese public's collective longing for his demise, which was long overdue. But, like the dreaded villains from Hollywood's popular horror films, he returned, time and again, looking healthier than ever, having received costly medical treatments at a Singaporean hospital or performed restorative cabalistic rituals at an undisclosed location. So, naturally, I treated the recent tidings of his death with a skeptic's reservation.

Eventually, when I consulted CNN and CBS, I realized Ne Win had indeed passed away. Isolated and ignominious, having been implicated in his kin's alleged plot to overthrow the ruling military regime (which was largely made up of his protégés), he spent his final days under house arrest. A mere shadow of the mighty despot he once was, he died

214 A Prayer for Burma

at the age of 92, on a December morning, at his lake-
side family villa. He was cremated on the same day,
devoid of the gregarious military exuberance he was
used to in life, and his ashes were tossed into a river.

Now, the survival of his surviving relatives
becomes highly questionable; his son-in-law and his
three grandsons have been tried for treason, con-
victed, and sentenced to hang. Many believe his
darling daughter, Sanda Win, will soon be charged
with the same crime and sent to join her husband
and sons in the notorious Ine Sein Jail, within whose
mossy walls thousands of dissident students and
democratic leaders are languishing in anonymity.

For his role in this alleged conspiracy, Ne Win's
soothsayer also received a 21-year prison sentence;
the government prosecutors' list of evidence included numerous voodoo dolls in the likeness of key
military officials, presumably to be used in conjunc-
tion with black magic. As fanciful as this might
seem to the outsiders, this hardly surprises those
who knew the former strongman. His preoccupa-
tion with astrology, numerology, and witchcraft was
legendary: he was rumored to regularly bathe in
dolphin blood to postpone his otherwise imminent
death; on his 90th birthday, his last public appearance, he offered lunch to 99 monks, befitting his
documented faith in the supernatural power of the
number 9.

Sadly, Ne Win's passing is hardly the answer to
Burma's prayer; there is still good reason to be skep-
tical about the country's future. So far, the military
regime that succeeded Ne Win is turning out to be
just as appalling, if not worse, and there's no sign
that it will give up its mulish obstinacy and thug-

gish ruthlessness—both ghostly reminders of Ne Win's own personality. The brilliance of the land of golden pagodas is still in the shadow of the Burmese Army's khaki gloom.

Identity, personal or national, is the product of freedom; no person or nation can fully establish an identity if it is denied the right to define its own personal and political destiny. I pray that Burma's identity crisis ends soon.

Kenneth Wong
San Francisco
January 2003

ORDER FORM 1-800-784-9553

	Quantity	Amount
Blues for Bird (epic poem about Charlie Parker) ($16.95)	_____	_____
The Book of Good Habits ($9.95)	_____	_____
The Butt Hello . . . and Other Ways My Cats Drive Me Crazy ($9.95)	_____	_____
Café Nation: Coffee Folklore, Magick and Divination ($9.95)	_____	_____
Discovering the History of Your House . . . ($14.95)	_____	_____
Exploring Our Lives: A Writing Handbook for Senior Adults ($14.95)	_____	_____
Footsteps in the Fog: Alfred Hitchcock's San Francisco ($24.95)	_____	_____
FREE Stuff & Good Deals for Folks over 50, 2nd Ed. ($12.95)	_____	_____
Jackson Pollock: Memories Arrested in Space ($14.95)	_____	_____
James Dean Died Here: America's Pop Culture Landmarks ($16.95)	_____	_____
How to Find Your Family Roots . . . ($14.95)	_____	_____
How to Speak Shakespeare ($16.95)	_____	_____
How to Win Lotteries, Sweepstakes, and Contests . . . ($14.95)	_____	_____
The Keystone Kid: Tales of Early Hollywood ($24.95)	_____	_____
Letter Writing Made Easy! ($12.95)	_____	_____
Letter Writing Made Easy! Volume 2 ($12.95)	_____	_____
Nancy Shavick's Tarot Universe ($15.95)	_____	_____
Offbeat Food ($19.95)	_____	_____
Offbeat Golf ($17.95)	_____	_____
Offbeat Marijuana ($19.95)	_____	_____
Offbeat Museums ($19.95)	_____	_____
Past Imperfect: Tracing Your Family Medical History ($12.95)	_____	_____
A Prayer for Burma ($14.95)	_____	_____
Quack! Tales of Medical Fraud ($19.95)	_____	_____
Redneck Haiku ($9.95)	_____	_____
The Seven Sacred Rites of Menarche ($11.95)	_____	_____
The Seven Sacred Rites of Menopause ($11.95)	_____	_____
Silent Echoes: Early Hollywood Through Buster Keaton ($24.95)	_____	_____
Tiki Road Trip ($16.95)	_____	_____
What's Buggin' You?: A Guide to Home Pest Control ($12.95)	_____	_____

	Subtotal _____
Shipping & Handling: 1 book $3.00 Each additional book is $ .50	CA residents add 8.25% sales tax _____ Shipping and Handling (see left) _____ TOTAL _____

Name _____

Address _____

City _____ State _____ Zip _____

❏ Visa ❏ MasterCard   Card No.: _____

Exp. Date _____ Signature _____

❏ Enclosed is my check or money order payable to:

Santa Monica Press LLC
P.O. Box 1076
Santa Monica, CA 90406

www.santamonicapress.com 1-800-784-955